THE FIRST BOOK OF
SMALL STOCK INVESTING

Grow Your Investment Portfolio by Investing in Small Capitalization Companies

SAMUEL CASE

Prima Publishing

PRIMA PUBLISHING and colophon are registered trademarks of Prima Communications, Inc.

Originally published by Prima Publishing as *Big Profits from Small Stocks.*

Library of Congress Cataloging-in-Publication Data

Case, Samuel.
    The first book of small stock investing: grow your investment portfolio by investing in small capitalization companies / Samuel Case.
      p. cm.
    Includes index.
    ISBN 0-7615-1439-2
    1. Small capitalization stocks—United States. I. Title.
HG4963.C374 1998
332.63'2044—dc21   98-15534
                                          CIP

98 99 00 01 HH 10 9 8 7 6 5 4 3 2 1

Printed in the United States of America

Investment decisions have certain inherent risks. Any investment a reader may make based on the information in this book must be at the reader's sole risk. You should carefully research or consult a qualified financial advisor before making any particular investment.

Furthermore, while efforts have been made to make this book complete and accurate as of the date of publication, in a time of rapid change, it is difficult to ensure that all information is entirely accurate, complete, or up-to-date. Although the publisher and the author cannot be liable for any inaccuracies or omissions in this book, they are always grateful for suggestions for improvement.

How to Order

Single copies may be ordered from Prima Publishing, P.O. Box 1260BK, Rocklin, CA 95677; telephone (916) 632-4400. Quantity discounts are also available. On your letterhead, include information concerning the intended use of the books and the number of books you wish to purchase.

Visit us online at www.primapublishing.com

CONTENTS

INTRODUCTION

Congratulations! By buying or borrowing this book, you have set yourself apart from the majority of investors. Your willingness to walk a different path can lead to much greater gains. If you take the information in this book to heart, you are likely to make a great deal of money.

Historically, many investors have been wary of small company stocks because of the risks involved. Reducing risk is the subject of one of my chapters, but let me say right now that the greatest factors in reducing risk are knowledge and awareness. Investing in small company stocks requires more time and study than putting your capital into a portfolio of mutual funds. Are the returns worth the hours and energy? One look at the charts in the first chapter should answer that question.

Taking this path requires not only a willingness to be different but also the willingness to spend some time researching a promising company and then keeping tabs on it after you buy its stock. But this work can be very rewarding—and not just monetarily. Investors in small companies often find themselves more involved in their investments than other investors. You may become fascinated by an exciting new product or service. You may find yourself calling up the company spokesperson with questions—or even advice. In short, you may find that investing has become a lot more fun.

So, dedicate your first study period to taking in the information in this book. It will provide the groundwork you need to invest in small companies. The fine newsletters recommended at the ends of various chapters will give you ongoing guidance. Basically, however, you're on your own in this field, and, if you are truly an individualistic investor, this is the way you like it.

This book is for people with some experience in investing. If you are a novice, I urge you to put this book on hold while you read my book for new investors, *The First Book of Investing*. It will give you the knowledge you need to begin investing successfully. Then you can read this book and start making even more money!

CHAPTER 1

WHY INVEST IN SMALL COMPANIES?

Why should you invest in small companies? Their fortunes go up and down, their products are often new and untried, and their management is typically composed of earnest, well-meaning young men and women with more enthusiasm than experience. These small firms are like boats tossed around by the financial winds compared with the grand ocean liners of the Fortune 500 corporations.

Quite simply, you should invest in small companies because they have been hands down the most successful investment category of the 20th century. At times, real estate in certain areas has done better; at other times, the blue-chip firms have topped the averages. Gold, silver, rare coins, even bonds, have all had their day. But one look at Table 1.1 on page 5 should convince you.

In 1940, $1,000 invested in the stocks of the big boys of the Standard & Poor's 500 would have turned into about $330,300 by 1991, with all interest and dividends

reinvested. But the same $1,000 put into small company stocks would have netted a total of $1,965,000 (see Table 1.1).

I hasten to point out that these figures are based on investing in *all* publicly traded small firms listed on the exchanges or the over-the-counter market. If you had carefully researched the most promising small companies and placed your capital only with them, you would almost certainly have done even better—a great deal better. I will discuss this kind of research in later chapters.

So read on. You will learn the best ways of researching and investing in small company stocks. If you put these methods into practice and the economy continues without a major breakdown, you're probably going to make a lot of money. You're probably also going to have a more interesting, exciting, and involving time than you would with a portfolio composed only of blue chips, bonds, and mutual funds.

TABLE 1.1 INVESTMENT RETURNS: 1940–1991

Asset Category	Compound Annual Return	Value of $1,000
Small-Cap Stocks	15.7%	$1,965,000
Large-Cap Stocks	11.8	330,300
Corporate Bonds	5.1	13,300
Government Bonds	4.8	11,400
Treasury Bills	4.3	8,900

Source: Roger G. Ibbotson and Rex Sinquefield, *Stocks, Bonds, Bills and Inflation: 1992 Yearbook.* (Chicago: Ibbotson Associates).

HISTORY LESSON

The historical record of the stock market contains a myriad of statistics showing the advantages of small stock investing, but Figure 1.1 displays most of what you need to know.

It's important to remember that the long-term advantages of small stocks as shown in this chart and others come from compounding the annual return, that is, reinvesting all gains. For example, since 1940, returns for large stocks have averaged 11.8 percent a year versus 15.7 percent for small stocks. This 33 percent difference doesn't seem that large until you look at the compounding charts in the Appendix. These charts reveal the dramatic difference between a return of 15.7 percent and 11.8 percent over a number of years.

THE FUTURE

Will the small stock advantage continue? During much of the 1980s, the blue chips of the S&P 500 outperformed the small stock averages. This was not an unusual occurrence.

FIGURE 1.1 SMALL STOCKS VERSUS LARGE STOCKS

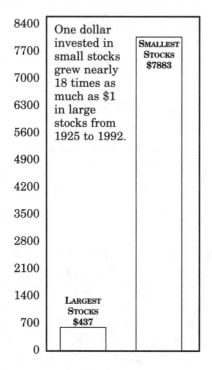

Source: Roger G. Ibbotson and Rex Sinquefield, *Stocks, Bonds, Bills and Inflation: 1992 Yearbook.* (Chicago: Ibbotson Associates).

The records show several such periods over the last six decades, but each time the small companies have reasserted their advantage.

The strength of the larger stocks during the 1980s was partly due to the popularity of *indexing* during that decade. Many large institutional investors and individuals bought portfolios or mutual funds that mimicked the stock indexes, and they generally chose the indexes that measure the performance of large companies. So they sold their shares in small firms and bought the large ones.

The early 1990s brought a dramatic rebound in the performance of small company stocks. In 1991, small companies outperformed their big brothers by 44 percent, in 1992, by 125 percent, and in 1993, by 141 percent.

During the great bull market of 1995–1997, the blue chips forged ahead. Small stocks lagged, but, if historical performance is any indicator, they may be ready to take the lead again.

From about 1975 up to the present, small companies have been the main engine powering the American economy. While many of the giant corporations have been downsizing and selling off assets, small firms have been providing much of the growth and many of the jobs in our economy. This trend should continue.

Therefore, in addition to the historical advantage, the present and the near future appear to be excellent times for investing in small companies.

Statistics are useful in showing the big picture. As was pointed out earlier, however, the statistics are for the entire population of small company stocks. By carefully choosing only the best companies, an individual investor should be able to substantially outperform the averages. And indeed, as we shall see in chapter 8, certain astute analysts have beaten the averages quite dramatically.

Before we get into how to select the best companies, though, let's look at a few more reasons why small companies will make your investment capital grow rapidly.

Scarcity Brings Value

In 1992, the stock of Whole Foods Market, a small natural foods company, stood at 10. By early 1998, investors had realized the value of this company and had driven the stock price up to 50.

Now there are two important factors in this stock's dramatic appreciation. The first is investors' belief that the company is well-positioned to take advantage of the growing demand for natural foods. Indeed, Whole Foods, which we talk more about in later chapters, is now the largest natural foods market chain in the country, and is steadily increasing the number of its outlets.

The second factor is that Whole Foods, like most small firms, had only a limited number of common shares outstanding at the time. This means that investors wishing to buy are bidding for a relatively small number of shares. If you have ever watched an auction where the price of a desirable object was quickly bid up to dizzying heights, you know the rest of the story. The fewer the shares outstanding, the faster their value rises when investors become interested.

In addition to having a small number of shares outstanding, the management of a small firm typically owns a large percentage of the shares. This effectively reduces the number of shares being traded, making them even more valuable.

By sharp contrast, a large corporation like IBM, with its 250 million shares costing $100 each, is harder to move. In a very good year, with individuals and institutions investing hundreds of millions of dollars, IBM stock might go up 15 points to $115. This holds true for all the giant corporations: investor interest just doesn't translate into as great an appreciation in stock value as it does with smaller companies.

We can state this as a physical law: It's possible to raise a smaller object to greater heights more quickly than a larger object.

The Low Price of Stock

The stock of most small companies can be purchased at low prices. What this means is that an individual investor can buy a large number of shares for a relatively small amount of money. For $5,000, you could buy 100 shares of a $50 stock in a sizable corporation. The same $5,000, however, would get you 1,000 shares of a $5 stock.

What this means is a chance of greater appreciation. If the $50 stock should rise 10 points to $60, the value of your investment would rise by $1,000 to $6,000. If, however, your $5 stock should go up by only 2 points, your 1,000 shares would now be worth $7,000, a rise of $2,000.

And if, as so often happens with well-chosen investments, your small company's stock should rise over, say, two years to $10, your investment would be worth $10,000. It is extremely unlikely that a large corporation's stock would double in value over two years. The most you could hope for would be an increase of 50 percent; most investors would be delighted with that.

So here's another law: It's better to control a large amount of something small than a small amount of something large.

The Efficient Market

While we're making laws here, investors need to be aware of a theory which many people now consider to be on the level of a law. This is the "efficient market" theory, and its main proponent is the economist Burton Malkiel, who wrote a book in 1973 titled *A Random Walk down Wall Street.*

In this book and a revised edition in 1990, Malkiel observed that the portfolios of the great majority of professional money managers didn't even keep up with the market. Two-thirds of these supposed experts on choosing the best stocks were outperformed by the S&P 500 Index during the 1970s and 1980s.

Malkiel believes that the reason for this is that in this age of instant communication, the investment community acts so quickly on any information about a company that most investors, whether institutional or individual, cannot profit from it. The stock rises or falls before they can buy or sell it.

This theory contains some large loopholes, and small company stocks charge through the largest one. Very few analysts are tracking and reporting on these smaller stocks. While there may be analysts in 20 major brokerages writing about any one of the S&P 500 corporations, there may be only two or three lesser-known analysts covering a small company. Sometimes there is only one—or occasionally none.

This means that a significant proportion of the investment community is unaware of many small companies, particularly the smallest ones. The lack of awareness is generally coupled with a lack of interest in small, struggling firms. "Too risky, too much trouble," is the usual assessment. Most investors would rather read about General Electric's chances of opening markets in Eastern Europe.

With fewer investors aware of a small company, its stock will tend to remain low. The large, institutional investors contribute to this neglect. Institutions are generally uninterested in small stocks until they reach a greater level of earnings and capitalization.

Most small company mutual funds, for example, will not invest in companies whose total market value is under $50 million. What this means is that hundreds of worthy companies are likely to be underfunded as well as underfollowed.

This situation creates a sterling opportunity for those willing to look at smaller companies. For example, a small firm may be working on a promising drug for treating cancer, but no one except a few insiders knows about it. Then, after a few years of research, the FDA approves clinical trials of the new drug and everybody wants a piece of the action.

The minute the FDA becomes involved, it's national news and the efficient market theory comes into play. The stock skyrockets, and it's too late for most investors to make good money on it. Only those who invested when the stock was selling for pennies will see a large profit.

THE CLUED-IN INVESTOR

Who are these astute investors and how can you become one of them? They come from essentially two groups. First, there are those who know about the field of cancer research—health-care professionals and interested laypeople. These people recognize the potential value of the drug being researched. The next chapter will look at investing in the fields of your own expertise.

The second group is made up of investors who heard about the company from friends as well as the few analysts who wrote about the stock. Subscribing to a few of the small company newsletters mentioned in this book will make you a member of this second group.

Both groups of investors also have the qualities of courage and patience—the courage to risk capital on a promising but unproven treatment and the patience to wait while the drug is being studied. Of course, such situations always entail some risk; ways of minimizing this risk will be explored in chapter 3.

In the meantime, the process of involving yourself in your investments—besides providing personal satisfaction and heightened interest—is also an excellent way to reduce risk. The more you know about what you're getting into, the less likely you are to misstep (that's yet another law).

Personal Involvement

In the 17th century, when people first began to invest in publicly owned companies, the investors usually knew the company owners. Before there were stock brokerages,

wealthy men used to meet each other in the coffeehouses of London and Amsterdam to discuss the latest enterprises—the East India tea trade, the fur business in the New World. Shipowners and entrepreneurs were likely to find interested friends or acquaintances with money to place in commercial endeavors.

Early investors usually took a personal interest in the companies where they put their money. The informality of the situation caused investor and entrepreneur to become more like business partners, discussing the company's problems over coffee. In short, investing was a more engaging pursuit in those days.

Placing your capital with small firms allows you to recapture some of that early spirit. A small firm may be pioneering an exciting new product that captures your imagination, or you may have become interested because a company's product or service is in a field about which you are knowledgeable. Even if you originally invested just because the company's financial picture looked good, your interest in its business may grow as you learn more about it.

However it happens, there is a much better chance that you will come to feel involved with a small firm than with a giant corporation. In these days, when investing is often done by the numbers, personal involvement can be deeply satisfying.

Personal Contact

Do you know something about a particular business? Call up a company doing this type of work, and offer some advice. Or do you simply want to know why its new line of goods has been kept from the market? Even small firms employ an investor relations director whose job it is to talk to you. You can get to know this person and keep in touch with him or her. You will probably find such exchanges not only rewarding but much more friendly and informal than communications with large firms.

As an investor in a small company, you are an important person. Your several thousand dollars' worth of stock represents a much larger percentage of the company than it would in a large corporation. So, not only may your contact at the company enjoy speaking with you, he or she is aware of your importance to the firm—and probably hopes you will invest more money or talk to your friends about investing.

If you live in the area where the company is located or find yourself nearby while traveling, pay a visit. Meet the managers and get a firsthand view of how they conduct business. This interaction will let you experience the kind of personal involvement investors used to enjoy.

But whether you can visit or not, learning about the business and speaking with the managers can be interesting and involving. Moreover, it can give you a much better feel for the firm's prospects. Peter Lynch, the former manager of the highly successful Fidelity Magellan Fund, talks about "immersing" himself in a company before he invests by learning as much as possible about the field it is in as well as about the company itself.

Investing with involvement can be much more rewarding both financially and intellectually than simply investing by the numbers. You need to remember the numbers, too, of course, but they are only part of the picture. Too many investors forget that companies are made up of real people and real products. It's easier to sense this when investing in small companies.

CHAPTER 2

HOW TO FIND THE BEST COMPANIES

This chapter deals with ways of finding the small companies that are likely to grow the most during the coming years. But first, I want to clarify a few terms, including *small*. The word means different things to different analysts. Just how small is small, anyway?

One generally accepted definition of small applies to the smallest 20 percent of stocks on the New York Stock Exchange in terms of *market capitalization*. This term refers to the market price of a company's stock multiplied by the number of shares outstanding, or the total value of all its shares. The firms in the smallest 20% generally have total capitalizations of less than $100 million.

It's important to note that this 20 percent refers to the New York Stock Exchange, which is generally where the big boys hang out. Sixty percent of the NASDAQ (National Association of Securities Dealers Automated Quotation System) market stocks fall into this category with a market cap below $100 million, as do 75 percent on the

American Stock Exchange. This means that almost half of the most frequently traded companies fall into the "small" category!

These figures don't include many thousands of small companies trading in the over-the-counter (OTC) markets. You will not see these firms listed in the stock pages of your daily newspaper, though many will appear in the listings of stocks on your personal computer (see Chapter 6). NASADQ has set up a special category for 6,200 OTC companies called the Bulletin Board.

A SMALL DIFFERENCE

Although *small cap* and *small company* have come to be used interchangeably, the terms are not equivalent. Because *cap* refers to the total capitalization of a company— the share price times the number of outstanding shares—some fairly large corporations fall in this category. If its share prices are depressed, a big company's total cap will be small. Before the airline company Pan Am finally went bankrupt in 1991, its share price was down to $1/4$. This was an extreme case, of course, but the point is that small cap does not always equal small company.

In addition, the definition of small company is often stretched by the mutual funds. So-called small company mutual funds often buy stocks in the medium range of capitalization, i.e., up to $500 million. So the term *small company fund* actually covers a lot of ground. Some such funds invest in small-growth stocks, others invest in undervalued companies (small caps instead of small companies), and still others are index funds.

You could put your money in good small company funds and probably do quite well. You would take advantage of the superiority of small stocks as shown in the charts of the previous chapter. Over the years, you could reasonably expect average returns of about 15 percent a year on your invested capital, maybe a little more. These are worthy returns. If you can achieve this percentage on the bulk of your portfolio, you are doing very well.

There are numerous ways to get a 15 percent return on your money, and there are several hundred titles on the book market that will tell you how to do it. In the case of small companies, however, it is possible to achieve even higher returns.

Those who want to put a little more time into their investing can do much better than average. The returns from individual small company stocks might give you double that of the mutual funds. However, you must do some research to find the small firms that are on the road to becoming large corporations.

INVESTING IN YOUR OWN BACKYARD

A successful writer and teacher of writing once advised me: "Write from your own backyard." In other words, use your experience to write what you know best. If this is impossible, the next best thing is to immerse yourself in the subject—to *make* it into your own "backyard."

Investors should take heed of this advice. You might think that you should always defer to the superior knowledge of investment professionals, but, in fact, you are probably an expert on at least a few subjects which a broker may know little or nothing about. In addition to your profession, you may have hobbies or other interests about which you know a good deal.

These areas of expertise are the first places you should consider putting your money. Are you in health care? Whichever branch of this large field you work in, you probably have knowledge or information which the general public does not. If your specialty is working with the physically disabled, for example, you are bound to be aware of the best new prosthetic devices coming on the market. Which companies are making these devices? Are these companies publicly traded? If they are, the next step is to call them and ask for their financial reports and any other information they can send.

For several years in the 1970s, I designed and built solar heating systems. At that time, my interest expanded to cover the entire field of environmentalism. When I became an investment adviser, I carried my knowledge of the environment with me and eventually started an investment newsletter that profiles small companies whose products help solve environmental problems. Chapter 4 will have more about environmental investing, but at the moment I simply want to emphasize how natural it can be to turn knowledge of a field into profitable investments.

Serious Interest

As an investment adviser, I often find myself encouraging clients to take their interests seriously. Recently, I counseled a client, Dan, whose hobby was repairing and flying antique airplanes. In this case, the investment opportunity came not from the airplanes themselves, but from the small airport where he kept the planes. A share in the general partnership that owned and managed the airport was up for sale. Dan had thought about buying in but didn't consider himself enough of an investment "expert" to do it. In other words, he didn't take his own expertise seriously.

The numbers looked very good to me. Not only did Dan receive a substantial reduction on his hangar rental, he got a tax reduction in the form of depreciation on his share of the property. Added to this was the increasing popularity of the airport, which had raised the value of shares during the previous several years. I urged him to approach the investment earnestly, talk to other shareholders, talk to the general partner, and look at the financial statements.

Not only are you two steps ahead if you're familiar with a certain field, you are also likely to take a greater interest if you enjoy the business in which you're investing. In Dan's case, for example, he would stay involved with the airport because his prize airplanes were there. This idea can be expressed as an equation: Greater interest equals greater involvement equals greater potential profit.

Expanding Your Network

Your friends and associates have their own vocations and avocations. If some of these people are investment-minded, you can trade information. Find out whether they know of any interesting companies in their fields of interest.

If you want to further expand your investment contacts, there are many investment clubs whose members gather to trade information and/or pool their money and invest together. Membership is a sterling opportunity to learn about more small companies.

The National Association of Investors Corporation (NAIC) is an organization of 7,500 investment clubs. Membership will give you information on clubs in your area. Particulars on how to join are in the Resources section at the end of this chapter.

Newsletters

Almost as good as personal knowledge of a field is listening to an expert whom you trust. Some editors of investment newsletters have track records in searching out the most promising small companies that make them worthy of your trust.

The accepted rates of return on most investments pale in comparison to the performance of the small-stock portfolios of the best newsletters. Generally, investors think that an average yearly return of 10 to 15 percent on capital is good, while 15 to 20 percent is excellent. But the returns on the stocks recommended by these publications are in another league entirely.

Among the top small-stock letters, an annual increase in value of 20 to 30 percent is not uncommon, and several have shown even better returns. These are not flash-in-the-pan performances either. Year in and year out, the returns come rolling in. In spite of this, year in and year out, most major investment firms and professional advisers dismiss individual small companies as too risky for the average investor.

Suffice it to say that an average return of 25 percent over a number of years puts to shame the common belief that small-cap stocks are "too risky." Check out the newsletters profiled in the various Resources sections, and decide for yourself.

While the recommendations of the newsletter analysts are an excellent start, you will still need to do some legwork before you buy. If you subscribe to several small-cap newsletters, you are going to find yourself with a slew of possible companies for investment. Pick out the stocks that most appeal to you, and then do your own research. This process is outlined in the upcoming section titled "Call 'Em Up."

Newspapers and Magazines

One excellent—and easy—way to find promising small firms is to read the business section of your local newspaper. You will often see stories about local businesses, especially if the firm is doing something new and unusual. Does the company have an exciting new product line? Is it about to issue stock? Has a shrewd and experienced CEO just been hired? These kinds of stories should make you sit up and take notice.

Finding a promising local firm is another way of investing in your own backyard. Perhaps you have a friend or acquaintance who works for this company, or you may know someone who does business with the firm. In any case, if you get interested, it will be easy to visit for a first-hand look.

Magazines can also provide information about small companies; look especially at magazines that deal with subjects of interest to you. Magazine editors love to include articles on new products and services, and usually behind these innovations is a new small company producing them. If you already know about the field, you are in a good position to judge whether a new idea has merit.

CALL 'EM UP

Once you find a company that interests you, phone to ask for its "financials," that is, its financial reports for the last two years and for the latest quarter (the 10K and the 10Q reports, respectively). Ask also for the latest annual report and for any other information the company is willing to send out—brochures, press releases, analyses by financial writers. This latter kind of information will, of course, be self-serving, but it can still help you to gain a better picture of the company's activities.

The 10K and 10Q reports tend to be thick and full of financial jargon. Much of the information you want will be contained in the financial statements, that is, the balance sheet and the income sheet (also known as the statement of operations). Chapter 10 offers sample financial statements and information on how to interpret them. That chapter also shows you how to set up a financial profile of a firm, using the information in the reports.

As for the rest of the facts in these reports, a company's annual report is a more readable source for the same information. Since this report is sent to shareholders, it is written in English instead of financialese.

You will need to start a folder or file for each company you research. This puts all the information in one place where it will be readily available. If you buy into a company, keep the file and simply add to it as more information comes in. This will be invaluable to deciding when to sell or, perhaps, whether to buy additional stock.

Supplementing any information you receive from the company, your brokerage will send you Standard & Poor's Stock Reports on most small companies. Some brokers give out these one-page reports for free, while others charge a small fee.

A Standard & Poor's Research Report is a detailed analysis that includes statistics, recommendations, earnings forecasts, and important developments relating to the company. These seven-page reports cost $5 each, but it's worth spending the money to get a disinterested analysis.

If the firm you are following is only a few years old and still very small, there's a good chance that S&P won't yet have a Research Report on it. But if they do, get it. You need to gather all the information you can about any firm you are thinking of buying into.

As you read the brochures and financial reports, write down any questions that occur to you. Then, when you're ready, call the company again and ask for the person in charge of investor relations. This person will answer your questions—and give you plenty of unsolicited information to boot. Naturally, this information is going to be slanted, but listen anyway. The people in the investor relations department are usually experts not only on their company but on the entire industry. You can learn a great deal by listening and asking questions.

All this may sound like a lot of work, but as you learn what to do, it will go quickly. Assuming you're familiar with the industry, learning everything you need to know

Market Share

One important piece of information you must find is the total market of the industry in which a given company operates. Next you need to learn how much of this market your proposed company controls at present. This will give you some idea of how large the firm might become. Question the director of investor relations about the company's plans to increase its market share.

One of the beauties of investing in small companies is that you occasionally find yourself investing in a new, expanding market, such as the market for environmental products (see chapter 4). In this case, a company's opportunities for growth far exceed those of firms in established markets.

---

about a particular company doesn't have to take more than a few hours, and the time spent will be rewarding.

By learning all you can before you put down any money, you place yourself far ahead of the 90 percent of investors who don't take the time to study. This means that, combined with the natural advantages of small company stocks, you will probably get a return several times higher than most investors achieve.

WHAT TO LOOK FOR

Product

One thing you're seeking through your research are firms with exciting new products or services. These could be brand-new start-up companies or older companies with new ideas. In some cases, an improvement on an existing product is extreme enough that it shows the same kind of promise as something new.

Occasionally you will find a company with an original marketing concept. For example, in 1988, a start-up firm called Grow Biz began buying and selling new *and used* sporting goods in its Play It Again Sports stores. This practice meant that their prices were often even lower than those of the big warehouse-type chain stores. In 1994, Grow Biz topped *Inc.* magazine's list of the 100 fastest-growing small public companies in the United States, with sales of $51 million. All this from a simple new concept.

Chapter 4 cites a company that is marketing a revolutionary method of packaging. The new product has many advantages over existing packaging material, not the least of which is that it's reusable. This is such a new concept in the field, in fact, that the company has been having trouble marketing it. Yet the product has so many good qualities that it's hard to imagine it won't eventually prevail. Whether this particular firm will prevail with it, however, depends on a few other factors, the most important of which is management.

Management

An innovative product or service that fills an important need matched with a skilled management team is an unbeatable combination. To bring a new product to the market, all the components of a company must work together—the production workers, the technical team, the marketing staff, and the managers, who must see that everyone is cooperating and working at top efficiency. In addition, the managers must have expert knowledge of the field and a feel for the best ways of bringing the product to the attention of prospective clients. And, last but not least, they have to be proficient at raising capital.

How can you tell if the people on the management team know what they're doing? First, look at their records. The information packet you receive from a company will provide descriptions of the top managers, including their experience in the industry and the skills they bring to their positions.

Second, if you feel the need to talk to any of the managers, call them up. Phone the vice president in charge of marketing and ask about the marketing stategy. Call up the technical director and ask if all the bugs have been worked out of the product. You're listening for more than the answers to your specific questions. You're trying to get a sense of whether they are really on top of what they're doing, whether they are committed to it and excited by it.

Financials

Now look at the results of the managers' efforts. Has substantial new capital been raised during the last few years? Do the balance sheets show greater profits or a definite movement toward profitability? Draw up your financial profile of the company as described in chapter 10, and study it carefully. Remember, even if a firm is not yet profitable, as long as it is moving strongly in that direction, it may be worth a good look.

Niche Markets

Inc. magazine specializes in small firms. It is the *Fortune* for small companies. Most of the companies profiled in *Inc.* are not publicly owned, so you can't buy stock in them, but once a year, the magazine publishes an article on the United States' 100 fastest-growing small public companies. The qualities that make a firm successful, of course, are the same whether it is privately owned or publicly held. And the phrase you see again and again while reading *Inc.* is "niche marketing."

If you are General Electric, you can afford to spread into many different areas. If, however, a firm's annual earnings are in the realm of $2 million, then it had better concentrate all its time, energy, and capital on one small piece of one market, and try to do it better than anybody else.

You are looking for whatever makes a certain company special; this could be either the product or the way the firm is marketing it. Second on the *Inc.* 100 list for 1994 was a new chain restaurant called The Lone Star Steakhouse and Saloon. Steak dinners are not new, but this successful niche market involves selling high-quality dinners at reasonable prices in a pleasant atmosphere.

PairGain Technologies (number three on the *Inc.* 100 list) makes specialized equipment that allows fiber-optic phone lines to be brought into all homes. This is a narrow niche, but there is enough of a market to facilitate extremely rapid growth. Revenues were $183,000 in 1989 and $36 million in 1993.

In this case, the opportunity—and the niche—opened up because of new technology. The *Inc.* list is packed with companies filling a need created by new technologies, particularly in information technology and networking. On the other hand, Lone Star and Grow Biz (the sports store selling secondhand and new goods) essentially created niches of their own by presenting quality, low-priced goods to the public.

So always define the niche that your prospective small company is aiming for. And, of course, try to satisfy yourself that the management is going about filling that niche in the most clever way possible.

Insider Holdings

One important item you want to find in a company's 10K report is the amount of stock held by the managers—the insiders. Often the managers will hold 25 to 35 percent of the outstanding stock. This is a good sign; it means that they are not only committed to the well-being of the firm, they are bullish on its stock.

Many analysts will watch for insiders buying more stock in their company; if they see this happening, they will buy, too, or at least watch the company closely. Their reasoning is that no one is in a better position to know whether a firm is doing well than its managers. Conversely, when the management is selling, this is considered very bearish for a company's stock.

Be aware, however, that insider trading may indicate only that management is attempting to stabilize the price of the company's stock. Managers will often buy their firm's stock when it is falling—and sell when the stock is rising. They know wild swings in price tend to scare off investors, while a relatively stable price range encourages them.

Intuition

After talking to people at the company and reading the information packets, do you have a feeling that this firm is heading toward success? This feeling is less tangible but no less important than the facts and figures on the balance sheet. You should be convinced that a company is on the road to prosperity before you invest in it. After doing all the necessary research, your intuition needs to give the final OK.

No Profits = Greater Opportunities

Many investors will not touch a company's stock until the balance sheet shows a profit. This reluctance means added opportunity for those willing to take a less rigid view. The companies I like the best are those that are not yet profitable but are moving in that direction.

Once a firm shows a profit, it attracts many more investors and the stock may rise sharply. I believe that a greater return can be realized by investing at the time when most of the company's income is going into research, development, and expansion.

This preference of mine, however, should not keep you away from promising firms with profitable balance sheets. Just remember that the reason you are investing in small companies is for growth—as much potential growth as you can detect.

GETTING YOUR FOOT IN THE DOOR

Suppose you like a company but don't feel ready to invest heavily in it. Perhaps you want to wait until new financing comes through, or maybe the product is terrific, but you don't feel totally confident about the managers. Here's what you do: buy only 100 shares of stock and wait before buying more.

As a shareholder, you will now be sent the quarterly and annual reports and, if you ask, all press releases issued by the company. You will be invited to attend the annual shareholders meeting, which is a useful thing to do if you live close enough to the company. In short, you are now an insider. When you call the information officer, you do so as a valued shareholder.

Owning even a small number of shares can change your attitude toward a company. You will probably find yourself becoming more interested in—and critical of—any new information about the company. Then, if you feel this information is positive and the elements that signal progress seem to be coming together, you can buy more shares.

Resources

National Association of Investors Corporation (NAIC), P.O. Box 220, Royal Oak, MI 48068-9972. Membership: $39/year. This includes a subscription to the monthly magazine *Better Investing,* and an Investors Manual, Club or Individual edition.

Hulbert Financial Digest*,* 316 Commerce St., Alexandria, VA 22314. (703) 683-5905. Monthly. $135/year. $37.50/five-month trial subscription.

Mark Hulbert analyzes the performance of investment newsletters. You have probably seen *Hulbert's* referred to in ads for newsletters: "Top rated by *Hulbert's.*" "In *Hulbert's* top five over the last three years." You can find ratings of newsletters in *Hulbert's* for different periods of time going back about 10 years.

Hulbert's includes various categories, and newsletters covering small company stocks is one. You can find the small-stock letters with the best annual returns, or at least some of them. *Hulbert's* is by no means comprehensive; for example, none of the four excellent newsletters whose editors are interviewed in chapter 8 is included. But if you feel the need to examine more publications than this book covers, *Hulbert's* is the place to look.

Select Information Exchange (SIE), 244 West 54th St., New York, NY 10019. (800) 743-9346. Get trial subscriptions to more small-stock newsletters than you can probably handle by contacting SIE. For a trivial fee (paid to SIE), this organization will contact a number of newsletters in any category you choose (small caps, blue chips, utilities, international, etc.) and tell the editors to send you free trial subscriptions.

Call the toll-free number and ask SIE to send you its information concerning small-stock newsletters. You will receive a long list with a short description of each newsletter, so you can select the ones you want. The fee depends on how many you choose. In a few weeks, you'll be inundated with more newsletters than you ever thought existed. From these, you can pick out a few outstanding ones that match your style of investing.

CHAPTER 3

HOW TO INVEST SAFELY

"There is no line of endeavor where real knowledge will pay as rich or quick a monetary reward as Wall Street."

—GERALD LOEB

I f I didn't know better, I'd say there was a conspiracy against small companies. Here we have a type of investment that has outperformed every other form of investment for the last 70 years and has brought enormous profits to most of the investors who used a little care and common sense. Granted, small companies have their ups and downs, but so does everything else.

The high returns from small company stocks more than offset their greater risk. Several investment studies have shown that, *even on a risk-adjusted basis,* gains from small company stocks are substantially greater than those from larger companies.

Despite this stellar record, when you mention small companies, most people draw in their breath through their teeth and shake their heads, saying, "Risky, risky! Didn't you hear about that company that went bust a couple of months ago? Better to stick with the blue chips." Numerous financial advisers and individual investors alike look down their noses at small company stocks.

Small company mutual funds have increased in popularity recently because of their excellent performance, but many people still shy away from individual small companies because they perceive great risk. Well, their loss is our gain.

WAYS TO MINIMIZE RISK

A few simple tactics will help you to dramatically lower your exposure to loss with small caps. These are easy to do and follow the rules of common sense.

Knowledge

In one sense, the pundits who warn against small company investing are right. If you were to invest the way most people do, which is often on a whim, while knowing very little about the company, then indeed you assume a great deal of risk.

Knowledge about your investments will set you apart from most investors. The research you need to do will not take a great deal of time, but it will ensure you a much greater return than most investors see. It may be that you will never be paid as well per hour as you will be when studying your small-cap investments.

Sadly, most investors do not take the time to do the necessary research before they buy, and this makes them more like gamblers than investors. When you are gambling, you are essentially paying for a dream. Buyers of lottery tickets, for example, are buying a fantasy of instant riches. People who buy stocks in companies about which they know nothing are doing the same thing: in this case, they are buying the fantasy that the stock will show a great increase in value. It's a fantasy because they have no facts to back it up.

If you don't want to spend any time doing research, you are better off in mutual funds. That way, you will be hiring the managers of the mutual funds to do the research for you. This can be a reasonable decision. Many people can't or don't want to take the time to concentrate on investments. Buying this book, however, places you in the category of investors who want to make their own choices and are willing to expend some energy doing it.

So the first, and most important, way to reduce your risk is to learn as much as you can about a company following the steps outlined in the previous chapter. Your research may not ensure success, but it will make it much more likely.

This risk reduction includes studying the industry in which a company works. I talked about investing in your own backyard—starting with your own fields of interest.

Temptations

Because we're human, we often act on impulse. It feels good: we're taking positive action, following our emotions, being decisive. When you're researching investments, the temptation is to jump in and buy when a firm looks good. Why wait?

You have all kinds of opportunities to be impulsive. Give somebody an unexpected hug. Take a day off and go hang gliding. But when you come down to earth, try to turn your impulse to buy into an impulse to learn everything you can about a company.

Impulsiveness can be expensive!

Another option is to look into a company that catches your eye and then learn all you can about the field it is in.

You need to know why the firm you are considering is special. What makes its product or service different or better than those of other companies in the field? It could be that this firm is simply operating with greater creativity and efficiency than the others, but you still need to know about the industry. Buying a dynamic small firm in a troubled industry often doesn't make sense.

Diversify

It's an unfortunate fact that even the most careful research is sometimes not enough. Many small firms have only one product or service, and if the demand should fall off, they and their investors are left high and dry. Similarly, if the economy should take a turn for the worse, revenues might be seriously reduced. Their size and limited scope make small companies more vulnerable to bad times than large corporations, whether the trouble is in their industry or in the national economy.

Investing in only one or two small companies is a good definition of a high-risk situation. The answer is to diversify. Don't spend all your money in one place. Spread it around!

Investing in 10 to 15 small companies means that if one or two should stumble, you'll still have a dozen others. And owning a large number increases your chances of finding the next Apple Computer.

In addition to diversifying among companies, you also need to diversify among industries. Don't put all your small-cap eggs in one industry basket, no matter how good it looks at the time.

When you have expertise in a field, it can seem natural to buy only in that area. But industries and economies change—sometimes too fast for buying and sell-

---

Temptations

It's tempting to put all your money in the one or two
stocks that look the best. Some companies look so terrific that it's hard to resist buying as much as you can.

Chapter 5 offers a couple of examples of firms that
seemed to have everything going for them and either
blew their opportunities or just didn't grow as fast as
other small firms. These are not unusual cases. Try to
remember them the next time a fantastic new product
marketed by a talented management team sweeps you
off your feet.

---

ing. If you own stocks in 15 companies, no more than five
should be in the same field. And you should own stocks in
at least three different industries.

Risk is laying all your hopes on one or two investments. Spread your money around!

Buy and Hold

I recently saw an article in a popular financial magazine
in which a couple was bemoaning the difficulty of investing in stocks. "After a few years of trying to guess what the
market was going to do, we just gave up and put our
money in mutual funds," they stated.

Indeed, trying to figure out what the stock market is
going to do has driven more than a few people out of the
market (and sometimes to drink). Besides being nerve-
racking, it's a lousy way to invest. There are a few (and
only a few) professional market "timers" who, with the
help of fancy charts, graphs, and computer programs, do a

fair job of predicting the general direction of the stock market. Amateurs might as well try to predict the future according to the stars.

Despite the difficulty, many people try to ride the ups and downs of the market. If you own mutual funds that invest in stocks and believe that the stock market is headed downhill, you can often switch your capital into a money market fund and try to ride out the downturn. When you believe that the market is going to rise again, you then switch your money back into the stock funds. Many mutual fund companies allow this switching at little or no cost.

One trouble with switching is that the market has a way of surprising even the professionals and "switchers" are often left behind as the market suddenly surges higher.

For individual-stock investors, particularly holders of a group of small company stocks, switching is not a rea-

sonable thing to do. The commissions to buy and sell the stocks are too high, and you run the risk of being out of the market when one or more of your stocks shows significant gains.

If watching the market is not a good option, though, what about watching individual stock performance day by day? Plenty of people do this: they are called *traders*. They will buy stocks they believe are poised to rise sharply in value. If the stocks do go up, the traders will sell them after a few days or weeks. If the stock starts to slide, they will sell immediately.

Trading requires three things: an excellent nervous system, quite a bit of expertise and experience, and a lot of time. It is a full-time occupation. This kind of speculation is not really gambling, although there are similarities. The professional trader has knowledge that raises his or her chances above those of the amateur. But attempting to be a trader without knowing what you are doing is definitely gambling. It's worse than gambling, in fact, because you have less chance of winning than you do in a casino.

This book is not about trading. But if you feel you want to give it a try, then, for heaven's sake, do it right. You can lose a tremendous amount of money if you don't. At the end of this chapter, you'll find the address of Jim Straw, a successful trader, businessman, and investor, who is also an excellent instructor. Ask for his list of publications, videos, and other offerings, so you can learn how and when to buy and sell.

The fundamental difference between traders and small-stock investors is this: Traders are looking for increases of at least 10 to 50 percent over a period of weeks. (They may or may not get it, and, of course, their gains may be offset by their losses.) As an investor in small stocks, you are looking for increases of 100 to 200 percent or more over a period of years. Occasionally, with a buy-and-hold strategy, you will find yourself holding a stock that just keeps on going up. Imagine having bought IBM

Temptations

Even if you've overcome any temptation to become a
trader, there's still the question of what to do when the
market takes a dive. It takes strong nerves to watch as
the value of your holdings slides into what looks like an
abyss. The impulse is to jump ship, forgetting that in a
storm you are much better on the ship than off it.
Through all the economic storms of the last 50 years,
the buy-and-hold investors have come out stronger than
ever. Remember that what goes down must come up!

---

or Xerox when they were small companies. Imagine how
you would feel if you had traded out of them early on for a
small profit!

Remember the chart in chapter 1, showing how small
stocks have performed over the years? That was a *buy-
and-hold* chart. You can reasonably expect those kinds of
increases if you hold onto your stocks for a few years.

Buying and holding not only gives you a better chance
of seeing large gains, it reduces your risk by a factor of at
least 10. Trading small company stocks is risk incarnate,
while buying and holding a portfolio of carefully chosen
small caps is hardly risky at all. This is because you are
prepared to sit out the inevitable ups and downs, and if
small caps continue as they have for decades, the overall
direction will be up.

How long you should hold depends partly on the performance of the stock. Chapter 11 will explore this decision in some detail.

To summarize, you can dramatically reduce your risk
with small caps if you behave as an investor rather than a
trader. Buy, and then sit tight for a long ride.

Balance

In spite of their excellent performance over time, small-cap stocks should make up only a portion of your investment portfolio. How large a portion is determined both by how much time you're willing to spend researching small companies and by your specific investment needs. If you're an experienced investor with time to spare and no need for extra income, you might place as much as 50 percent in small stocks. If, on the other hand, you are retired and need some income from your investments, you might keep only 10 to 20 percent in small caps.

My feeling is that you should have a maximum of half your investments in small companies. Yes, past returns have been excellent and the future looks promising, but looks have been deceptive in the past. Unforeseen events may affect the economy in coming decades, and when unusual events happen, you are almost always better off with a balanced footing.

In a major downturn, for example, small company stocks go down first and farthest. Income investments

Temptations

The temptation in this case is to put all your money in small-cap stocks. Their record is so good, so why not?

The point to remember here is that we really don't know what's going to happen in the world over the next 20 to 30 years. The rule that "past performance is no guarantee of future results" applies to the world economy and political scene just as it does to individual investments. A good balance is vital to being as secure as possible with your investments.

such as bonds and utilities, however, will remain much more stable. Blue-chip stocks tend to drop less and to revive sooner than those of small companies. Diversification into international stocks and bonds will give your portfolio even better balance.

Sadly, I often hear about unsophisticated investors who lost all their capital because they put it in one place. Too often, the place they chose—usually as a result of bad advice—was the futures or the options market. These are terrible places for most individual investors. But it's also possible to have too much of a good thing, even small stocks. Overinvesting in any single sector is a recipe for disaster.

So keep your investment capital safe by keeping your balance.

SAFETY WITH UNLISTED STOCKS

When a publicly owned company gets to be a certain size, it will usually apply to be listed on a stock exchange or on the National Association of Security Dealers Automated Quotation System, better known as NASDAQ. But before they are listed on an exchange or on NASDAQ, companies are traded in that vast, murky place known as the over-the-counter market. This market includes 6,200 small stocks whose bid and ask prices are carried on the NASDAQ Bulletin Board and 11,000 stocks on a competing service known as the Pink Sheets.

Buying an over-the-counter stock is as easy as buying a listed stock: you simply phone your broker. You should know, however, when you want to sell, that the market for unlisted stocks is often very thin; this means that they may be difficult to sell in any quantity. One great advantage of the listed stocks is that they almost always have a more liquid market.

The different exchanges and NASDAQ have various requirements for a company to be listed with them. A certain level of earnings, net worth, and a minimum share price are necessary. The New York Stock Exchange has the most strict requirements, NASDAQ and some of the regional exchanges, the least strict.

Many people steer clear of over-the-counter stocks because they haven't been approved by any organized market. And indeed, in the past, various scams and strange dealings have been associated with this market, although nowadays this is rare.

I don't believe in writing off any market out of hand. What you need to do with an over-the-counter company is simply apply the same risk management that you would use with any other small firm. Check out the administration, the product, and the financials. Look at the industry, the insider holdings, and the niche the company is aiming to fit. This is the kind of research that makes risk manageable when you're buying any small stock. You need to concentrate on the company itself, not the market it's in.

To buy only listed or NASDAQ stocks is to cut yourself off from some of the best opportunities. And because a company has fewer investors at this stage of its life, the stock price will probably be low, meaning that you can buy a larger piece of the company.

Another advantage to buying into an over-the-counter company on the rise is that eventually it will get itself listed on an organized market. When it does, if the company is continuing to do well, the stock will usually rise due to the added exposure to investors. In fact, this is a piece of information you need to research. Ask the managers about their plans for a listing. They will usually have projected a time frame for getting the firm listed on an exchange or on NASDAQ.

Resources

Phlander Company. P.O. Box 5385, Cleveland, TN 37320-5385.

If you're going to trade with even a portion of your portfolio, you absolutely need to know what you're doing. Write to Jim Straw at the Phlander Company and ask him for his publications on how to trade stocks.

CHAPTER 4

INVESTING IN THE ENVIRONMENT

T he promising small companies you discover will probably be spread over various industries. This is good. As was pointed out in the previous chapter, buying companies in a number of fields makes for healthy diversification.

Occasionally, however, one particular industry will stand out as a prime place to put your money. Consider, for example, the personal computer industry in the 1970s. Investors had a chance to get into fledgling businesses that were to become giant corporations. Many opportunities still arise in this industry because it is growing and changing so fast. But the opportunities were even greater 20 years ago when there were numerous start-up companies; an astute investor could have sorted out the best ones.

The question inevitably arises: is there an industry today positioned in roughly the same place as the computer industry was in the early 1970s? I believe there is and that it is the environmental field. This chapter is devoted to the growing number of companies whose products or services represent solutions to the pressing environmental problems of the day.

I am including this subject for two reasons. First, as an investor in small companies, you need to know where the greatest opportunities may be found. Second, becoming familiar with this growing field will allow you to extrapolate to other fields. Learning why environmental companies are coming into the forefront will enable you to recognize the signs when other industries are on the way to this favored position. In addition, I want to illustrate the many different sectors where promising companies can be found in a growing industry.

NATURE IN THE SPOTLIGHT

The environment is an urgent issue that's receiving attention because more and more people are finally realizing that polluting the world we depend on for our livelihood is a dangerous game. And, after years of foot-dragging by the federal government, more money is being appropriated to clean up our messes—and prevent new ones from being made.

This private and public interest creates a perfect climate for enterprising businesses with new and better solutions to ecological problems. These new ventures can be found in a variety of areas. Let's take a look at a few.

Waste Management

For years, all things that no one wanted anymore were simply hauled to the dump. Dumps proliferated and began to fill and overflow the areas allotted to them. Over time, the toxic elements in the waste piles leached through the soil and eventually into the groundwater—which often was part of the water supply for cities and farms. Not only was the environment close to the dumps becoming less pleasant, the dumps were becoming health hazards.

The Environmental Protection Agency has now placed much more stringent regulations on dumps and landfills. Unable to meet these requirements, many dumps are simply closing down. A few years ago, there were approximately 5,000 major landfills in the country. By the year 2000, there will be only 3,000.

With cities and industry casting about for new ways to deal with their waste, a whole new industry is growing around the concept of recycling. Several small, young firms are composting organic waste on a grand scale. Not only are they paid for accepting the waste, their end product is a fertilizer which they sell to organic farms and gardens. A few companies using this technology are already turning a profit; others are on the way.

This is just one example from the burgeoning field of recycling and waste management. New companies with solutions are appearing almost as quickly as new problems are identified.

Clean Transportation

Our industrial civilization has succeeded in badly polluting our air. The worst culprit is the internal-combustion engine, found in tens of millions of vehicles. This has been one of the most difficult environmental problems. People need the cars and trucks, but the exhaust they produce is toxic. Mass transit keeps many cars off the road, but it's not enough.

A solution to this problem is finally in the works, although it may take several decades to make a real difference. Vehicles propelled by electric motors have been around for a long time, but only now are they beginning to get the attention they deserve.

Electric vehicles are not only nonpolluting, they are quieter, function more efficiently, and require less maintenance than gasoline-powered cars and trucks. It is true that the electricity to charge the vehicles' batteries is produced in generating stations powered by fossil fuels, but the overall pollution is greatly reduced. In addition, more and more of the battery charging in the future can come from nonpolluting sources such as photovoltaic cells.

California and several other large states have mandated that, by 2003, 2 percent of all vehicles sold in their borders must be nonpolluting. Right now, the electric car is the only technology that fulfills this requirement.

At present, the major auto companies are beginning to market a few electric vehicles, but the only small companies producing electrics are mostly privately owned, meaning they don't sell stock. This could change radically in the next few years. Watch for small firms producing "hybrid vehicles"—electrics with a small gasoline engine to increase the range before needing to recharge. Also, watch for companies that produce components for electric and hybrid cars such as motors, control systems, and batteries. Batteries that can provide greater range for electrics are on the way.

Problems and Pioneers

The strength and scope of the environmental movement is such that it will affect our economy in many areas. Each area contains problems which entrepreneurs see as opportunities. Here are a few more environmental issues together with the kinds of companies coming up with solutions. An investor might want to look for such pioneering efforts.

Problem: Pesticides and chemical fertilizers are degrading the soil and putting toxic chemicals into our food.

Solution: Grow and market food cultivated with organic fertilizers and no pesticides.

Companies: A few publicly traded companies market organic food and work in related areas. The number is limited because the producers—the farms—don't sell stock.

Problem: Burning fossil fuel not only generates pollution, it is a finite resource and a cause of international tensions.

Solution: Encourage the use of nonpolluting renewable energy sources, such as sun and wind.

Companies: A growing number of firms are manufacturing photovoltaic cells, which produce electricity from sunlight. The cost of these cell modules has been going down each year and is already competitive with fossil fuels in certain applications. There are also some companies producing solar water heaters, a field with great growth potential. Moreover, electricity from windmills is successfully competing with fossil fuel plants in several areas of the country.

Problem: Present building methods and materials are increasingly expensive, energy-inefficient, and occasionally toxic. They can also strain such renewable resources as trees.

Solution: Employ innovative building materials and methods.

Companies: A small but growing number of firms produce and/or build with new, energy-efficient, nontoxic materials.

FINDING THE BEST

The environmental industry is growing in both size and breadth. As new environmental problems crop up, new technologies must be developed to deal with them. Getting involved in such a rapidly changing field can be exciting. You're on the forefront of new technologies that can help save the environment and improve our lives.

As we have seen, promising companies are often found on the periphery of a field. For example, the companies that produce improved energy-storage systems—batteries, flywheels, etc.—may grow even faster than the electric vehicle firms that employ the systems. In the field of organic food, one small publicly traded company has found its niche in supplying information to farmers on how to grow food organically. Investors who broaden their perspective when viewing an industry will often see things which other investors miss.

At the end of this chapter, you will find a list of several publications that will help you find the most promising environmental firms. These newsletters are the best places to start looking, but keep your eyes open in your area, too. You may discover a small environmental company opening for business just down the street.

Unlimited Opportunity

Most small companies belong to fields that have limited markets. If a product is good, skillful managers can maneuver a firm into a competitive position and garner a share of the total market. Because of the inevitable competition, however, the company will probably approach a ceiling at some point and cease to grow at a fast rate.

The field of the environment, however, is so new that new markets are continually being created. No one knows how large they can become, but if you choose a company with care, you might end up with one of the leaders—the next Microsoft of the environmental world. New companies and exciting new fields are a great combination for the small-cap investor, and I see environmentalism as the most exciting area right now.

Resources

New Energy Report, 84 Canyon Rd., Fairfax, CA 94930. (415) 459-2383. $60/year for six issues plus occasional special reports. $20/trial. Editor: Samuel Case (the author of this book).

The *New Energy Report* profiles promising small companies whose products or services address the great environmental problems of the day. These have included companies involved in electric vehicle manufacturing, waste recycling, natural foods, reusable packaging, waste heat recovery, and even environmentally friendly mining.

The Environmental Investor's Newsletter, 410 North Bronson Ave., Los Angeles, CA 90004-1903. (213) 466-3297, (800) 995-1903. Fax: (213) 465-9361. $59/year for six issues.

This publication features investment-ripe private and public companies in the pollution control, alternative energy, recycling, and biotechnology industries, and tracks about 100 environmental public stocks for socially responsible investors. More than 200 companies and funds have been profiled since its debut in September 1991.

The publisher, Chasen & Luck, also maintains the Environmental Investor Network, a direct-mail data base of more than 10,000 names, which links investors with public and private firms, limited partnerships, and joint venture opportunities.

The Greenmoney Journal, 608 West Glass Avenue, Spokane, WA 99205. (509) 328-1741. Quarterly. $35/year.

If you are serious about socially responsible investing, then you need this journal. Publisher and co-editor Cliff Feigenbaum has made *Greenmoney* into a real forum for concerned investors. There is a "Green News" section, a list of environmental publications, a "Green Events Calendar," and a performance update on social mutual funds, as well as excellent lead articles on the latest developments in the field. You will not find individual companies recommended, but you will gain an overview of the subject, which will direct you towards the promising areas for investment.

Since 1995, *Greenmoney* has had a Web site: http://www.greenmoney.com. This site has information similar to the newsletter, but is up-to-the-minute.

The Socially Responsible Guide to Smart Investing: Improve Your Portfolio As You Improve the Environment, by Samuel Case (the author of this book) Prima Publishing, 1996. $19.95 (hardcover).

There are two kinds of social investing. The first might be termed the "do no harm" method: investing in companies whose products and services do no harm to social or natural environments. The second is the "pro-active" method: putting your capital into firms that are actively working on environmental problems. *The Socially Responsible Guide* describes the best and safest ways to invest using both methods. The main focus of the book, however, is the growing field of environmental business. Investors are shown how to find the most promising companies involved in recycling, renewable energy, clean transportation, responsible waste disposal, and environmental merchandising.

CHAPTER 5

PICKING WINNERS:
A FEW CASE HISTORIES

W e're going to look at three small companies in this chapter. One of them is well on its way to success, another has stalled for a few years but may get moving soon, and the third has never delivered on its possibilities. All showed great promise at the start, but they have gone in radically different directions.

We will closely examine the reasons why these small firms have shown such divergent levels of success. This should help you learn what to watch for in a developing company.

These stories may also serve as a warning against overenthusiasm. The excitement of discovering a wonderful new product can influence your good judgment. But exciting new products are not enough; a market must exist for them. Then, if there is a market, they need to be sold in a clever and aggressive manner. There must be enough financing to keep the firm afloat and doing business, and, most critical, the management team must be experienced and skillful.

Thus, once again, the three main factors to study in any company are product, financing, and management. Let's see how these factors have influenced the success or failure of three innovative businesses.

WHOLE FOODS MARKET

We're going to look first at a small stock investor's dream: a small company that has grown large in just a few years. Whole Foods Market has it all: great management, popular products, and earnings which increase every quarter. Even though this company is fast becoming too large for small-cap investors, the lessons of its success are invaluable. We're going to follow the reasons for this success and these should aid you in finding other promising small companies.

A Natural Leader

The success of modern agriculture at growing large quantities of food is impressive. During the last two decades, however, the quality of the food and the methods used to grow it have been called into question. A growing number of consumers have become wary of the pesticides and herbicides used on crops of grains and produce, and these shoppers have moved towards food grown in a natural, chemical-free manner. Farmers and merchandisers of organically grown food have been rapidly expanding their businesses.

Whole Foods Market has placed itself at the forefront of this movement. Whole Foods started with one small natural foods store in Austin, Texas, in 1978. By 1980, they had opened their first supermarket under the name of Whole Foods Market. Over the next 10 years, 10 more supermarkets were added, mostly in Texas. Then, in January of 1992, the company went public, raising more than $22 million from the sale of common stock. A second offering followed in January of 1993.

Armed with the capital gained from these stock sales, Whole Foods went shopping. The company began to buy and merge with its competitors; in 1992 and 1993, three smaller natural food chains were incorporated into the company, giving Whole Foods a total of 30 stores—and a national presence. Since then, building and acquisition have brought the total to 82 stores in 22 states. Management plans to have 100 stores by the year 2000 and 140 by 2003.

Natural Products

A visit to a Whole Foods Market is a mind-expanding experience. The store in Mill Valley, California, is as large as any major supermarket. The bins are piled high with fresh organic produce; when the purchasers are unable to get organic fruits and vegetables they will buy non-organic varieties, but they label them clearly as such. Most of the meat and poultry comes from free-range animals raised without the use of hormones or other chemicals in the feed.

Vitamins and food supplements fill a large area, with numerous pamphlets instructing shoppers in their proper use. A delicatessen features Thai chicken salad, lowfat potato salad, and other gourmet items made from natural foods. Whole Foods has successfully merged natural foods with gourmet concepts; going organic no longer has to mean eating plain, unexciting food.

In addition to this bounty of organic foods, the shelves are filled with every manner of natural products, that is, fabricated with as few chemicals as possible. There are small instructional pamphlets placed near the various sections with titles like *Evaluating Pet Foods* or *A Pest-Free Yard. Looking Good!* describes the body-care products sold in the store: natural ingredients, no chemicals, and no animals employed in testing the products. Other pamphlets give more general instructions on such topics as composting or the healing power of food.

A Natural Mission

Educating consumers is an integral part of the Whole Foods experience. In addition to the pamphlets mentioned above, signs at various counters tell of the advantages of organically grown produce and chemical-free meats. This kind of instruction is, of course, good for business: to convince shoppers of the value of the products is to ensure that they will return for more.

But as you wander through the store and talk to some of the employees, you begin to realize that there is more going on here than smart merchandising. These people believe in what they're doing: they have a mission. For one thing, they are not called employees, but Team Members. Each person is an important part of a growing company. Even the Board of Directors calls itself a Team.

The sense of mission pervades the company from the top down. CEO John Mackey (one of the original founders) states the purpose of the company very clearly: "Our deepest purpose as an organization is helping support the health, well-being, and healing of both people (customers and Team Members) and of the planet (sustainable agriculture, organic production and environmental sensitivity)."

The recently adopted slogan for the company is "Whole Foods—Whole People—Whole Planet."

A strong sense of purpose, when combined with savvy management, can be a great recipe for success. Managers and workers who believe in their product are more likely to go the extra mile to grow the company. Bill Gates of Microsoft is another good example of this kind of dedication: he is a tireless advocate of computers—in the workplace, in the schools and in the home—and he has surrounded himself with like-minded people.

Enthusiasm is not enough in itself, of course; it must be coupled with skilled management practices—and in this Whole Foods has excelled.

How to Grow a Company

A growing number of companies, both large and small, are working on involving their employees at every level in the running of the business. At the same time, through employee stock option plans (ESOPs), these workers are included in the ownership and profits of the firm. This is good business: the firms that involve their employees seem to enjoy better than average success.

Whole Foods is a prime example. All Team Members are encouraged to contribute ideas at Team Meetings. Members are granted various kinds of options to purchase company stock, based on hours worked and promotions. These policies bear fruit in many ways, not the least of which is morale: ninety-five percent of Team Members have reported high to very high job satisfaction.

In 1992, in a dramatic move towards economic democracy, the directors decided that no one—not even the directors themselves—should earn more than 10 times the average, full-time Team Member pay. This is important, not just from the standpoint of economic justice and employee morale, but also for investors. Large executive salaries take away from the amount a company has to invest in its own development.

Investors' Heaven

The growth of Whole Foods provides several examples of what small stock investors need to look for in a company. At present, the company is growing its way out of the realm of small stocks, but a few years ago it would have been an excellent buy in that category. In 1993, when I first recommended the company to my clients, it was already showing rapid growth. The product—natural foods—was proving itself to be a winner with consumers, and management seemed to be skillfully maneuvering the company to take full advantage of this popularity. Earnings were growing steadily, the debt picture looked manageable, and the stock price was rising.

This last—the stock price—is especially instructive for investors. Like many growing companies, Whole Foods' stock price rose and fell like a bungee jumper. This volatility can discourage many investors, but it is part of the small company world. What was important was that the general trend was strongly upward. In May of 1993, the price stood at $18 (adjusting for splits). Over the next five years, in spite of dramatic rises and falls, the value had risen to $50 a share. Let's hear it for buying and holding! The investors who were scared off by the volatility and ignored the strong fundamentals of the company never got to enjoy the benefits.

What's Next

Whole Foods is still going strong; Standard & Poor's Stock Reports rate the stock as a five-star BUY. And, in spite of the costs associated with the rapid expansion, earnings continue to grow at a fast clip.

In September of 1997, the company merged with Amrion, a manufacturer of vitamins, herbs, and nutriceuticals, based in Boulder, Colorado. And a specialty food retailer called Merchant of Vino was acquired at the end of 1997. This six-store chain, located in the greater Detroit area, is not a natural products store, but Whole Foods management wanted to expand into new areas.

Just to give an idea of the growing diversity of the company, at the end of 1997, Whole Foods operated 82 stores, 7 distribution centers, 8 regional bakehouses, 3 commissary kitchens, a seafood processing facility, a produce field inspection office, and a manufacturing distribution center of nutritional supplements. The firm employs over 11,000 people nationwide. The present stores average 24,000 square feet in size and $14 million in annual sales. The stores in development are larger, measuring 30,000 to 40,000 square feet.

Small companies need to keep a pretty narrow focus; they need to find their niche market and try to be the best in that niche. But success and greater size usually lead to diversification into related fields.

Competition is growing, as conventional supermarket chains attempt to cash in on the natural foods trend. In the Boston area, for example, where the company stores are called Bread & Circus Whole Foods, four large, new natural foods stores opened in 1997. In spite of this competition, however, sales for the Bread & Circus stores grew by 9 percent in 1997. So far, Whole Foods is the largest in its field and has managed to outdistance the competition.

The lesson here for small stock investors is that when you match great products that are growing in popularity with excellent management, you will almost always have a winner. And if you have strong motivation and morale among the workforce, this is another large plus. Even though Whole Foods is no longer a small company, you, as an investor, can use its success as a prime example of what to look for in newer small firms.

AIR PACKAGING TECHNOLOGIES

Growth in fits and starts is usually the rule for small companies. Sometimes they will lie dormant for years and then a change in the market or management will propel them into rapid development. In the case of Whole Foods Market, both of these factors changed quickly, catalyzing the company's growth.

Meanwhile, other small companies are just starting up. Let's look now at a small start-up offering a product with tremendous potential. This company has been struggling for all of its short life, and, while it has finally found a niche market, the financial reports are still nothing to write home about. Nevertheless, the product's dramatic possibilities make this the kind of company that investors will want to watch closely.

In 1986, company founder-to-be Dan Pharo visited a friend's child in the hospital, bringing him a small toy truck. On a whim, instead of gift wrapping the truck, Pharo inserted it inside a balloon and blew up the balloon. The truck with its novel wrapping was an instant hit, and Pharo realized that he might have a salable product.

Soon he was marketing inflatable air bags with colorful designs as a new kind of gift wrap. Insert a toy, inflate the bag, and you had a novel wrapping that required no boxes, ribbons, or paper. The bags sold well, but by 1989, Pharo had invented an improved, double-walled, inflatable bag. With this, he realized that he had a new method of packaging products for industry.

By the end of 1989, the company (based in Valencia, California) had reorganized and gone public on the Vancouver Stock Exchange. It began to manufacture and market the double-walled bags for industry.

Reduce, Reuse, and Recycle

The "air boxes" are a beautiful solution to a knotty problem. American industry uses a tremendous quantity of so-called interior packaging materials, designed to protect and cushion products during transportation. The packaging materials, however, create a raft of problems for the users; first among these is the materials' high cost, which stems from the great quantity of raw matter and energy necessary to fabricate them. Then, there is the time, energy, and space needed to convey, handle, and store them.

Packaging materials also create problems for consumers. Remember the last time you had to dispose of a large piece of hard, molded foam or a pile of messy polystyrene "peanuts"? They probably took up a good portion of the space in your trash can, and this space consumption continues when they get to the dump. These types of products take up 30 percent of the space in our landfills—the same landfills that are steadily shutting down all across the country. Major environmental problems are clearly associated with the packaging materials now in use.

Air boxes solve many of these problems. Fabricated from thin plastic film, they resemble freezer bags. Manufacturing them requires a great deal less energy and materials, they are easily transported and stored, and many of them are reusable. The receiver simply deflates them and removes the products; the air boxes are then ready to be used again. If they must be disposed of, deflated air boxes take up one-tenth of the space of the usual packaging materials.

The air box has received serious attention in the industry, regularly winning prizes for innovation and environmental packaging at exhibitions and trade shows. So far, however, this attention has not translated itself into the kind of business Air Packaging Technologies (APT) needs to grow and show profitability.

Past Struggles

Starting in 1989, APT had difficulty with its production of air bags. At first, quality control was an issue; later, when that was solved, quantity became critical. Orders were coming in, but the subcontractor fabricating the bags was falling far behind schedule. Unable to ship the product to distributors, the company incurred large losses and by fall 1991 was near to closing down. At this point, the firm itself took over the fabrication of the bags and new financing was found, so APT managed to survive.

In May 1992, the company took delivery of a second-generation production machine and, in a few months, was making 80,000 bags a day. Back orders and new orders were filled, and, for a time, the situation looked better.

In 1993, however, a fresh problem appeared. The new orders coming in were insufficient to fuel continued growth. This difficulty centered around industry's slowness to accept a radical new packaging concept. The managers had learned that this reluctance could be overcome by proper education and sales programs. Indeed, they had formulated several creative programs but lacked the capital to implement them.

By 1998, APT had finally succeeded in educating many computer and electronics firms about the advantages of the air box. These firms constitute a growing niche market for the product; sales are increasing and new contracts are in the works. Now, under new management, things are looking up for this small company. And, as the air box becomes better known, its use may expand to other industries.

The Glimmering Future

It is at this point in the short history of the company that an investor should begin to feel seriously interested. The product, innovative and exciting from the start, has been improved, and several new lines have been introduced to good effect. Quality control has been resolved, as has the problem with production quantity. The education and sales programs have born fruit.

As a potential investor, you need to keep a close eye on any company at this stage of development. Is there indeed a change of management? Does new capital appear during the next few months? Are there other changes in management that look positive? Is the firm signing new contracts with distributors? Positive answers to all these questions mean that you want to think about putting some serious money into the company.

There is an important period of transition in the life of most companies. This is the time when a small mom-and-pop business develops a more sophisticated corporate style of management and operations. This is also the time when the founder often bows out or recedes into the background, and the transition is, unfortunately, not always accomplished without acrimony and bad feelings. Many founders are just not ready to give up the reins.

In the case of Air Packaging, this transition has taken place. While Whole Foods Market management retains two of the three original founders—one is CEO—the management structure has gone through extensive changes and revisions. Our third company, Super Panels, has never gone through this kind of change, and perhaps never will.

In spite of the difficulties involved in such transitions, this change in management is frequently critical to the continued growth and success of a company. The pioneering skills and vision necessary to launching a new business are usually not the same skills and vision necessary to leading it to new heights. The new managers must be able to inspire cooperation and effort among the employees, market the product, and raise capital.

Investors should sit up and take notice during these times of transition. Change in itself, of course, does not guarantee success. Whether the changes are going to work will only become apparent during the following year or two. If the company seems to be headed in a successful new direction, this is the time to invest.

If you have watched the signs closely, you will often be able to buy before the stock rises significantly. But even if you miss the lowest prices, an expanding small company with a great product and good management is a gem: put your money into it and keep it there for a long time.

SUPER PANELS BUILDING SYSTEMS

The building industry is ready for some innovation (many would say it's long overdue). Scientists are on the point of building a space station, using all sorts of advanced materials and techniques, while back here on earth, stud-wall construction is still the norm. The time is ripe for change, both in ways of reducing cost and in ease of construction.

This is why many people, including myself, were very interested a few years ago in a small company called Super Panels Building Systems. The folks at Super Panels had perfected an integrated building panel that required no framing. A honeycomb core is faced with exterior paneling on one side, interior paneling on the other, and insulation in the middle. The resultant wall's load-bearing exceeds that of conventional walls, and it has excellent resistance to fire, fungus, and moisture.

The founder of Super Panels had been building houses with these panels for 15 years and had managed to get them approved as a complete system by the U.S. Department of Housing and Urban Development, the state of California, and even the city of Los Angeles (which has stringent requirements for earthquake safety).

As if all this weren't enough, a builder using the panels was supposed to be able to put up a house in one-third the time at one-half the cost. Was it any wonder that many investors grew interested, despite the fact that the market for the stock was still very small?

How Not to Grow a Company

Around March 1989, when stock in Super Panels was selling for 10 cents a share, it began to attract more and bigger investors, and by December, the price was up to 75 cents. With talk of large contracts and new opportunities, most people believed that the company was ready to take off, along with the value of the stock. Instead, the price stayed in the 50- to 75-cent range for about a year and then began to drop. Today it's worth about 2 cents a share and is hardly traded at all.

What happened? Did all the homes constructed with Super Panels collapse in the Los Angeles earthquake? Nothing so drastic. What happened was . . . nothing: no great new contracts, no large increase in sales, no dramatic rise in the stock price.

The management of Super Panels, it seemed, was simply not up to the task of turning the firm into a growing, thriving corporation. For 15 years, the company had been using the panels to build houses; that was what the managers were used to doing and that was what they wanted to continue doing.

Several large investors endeavored to bring about change in the company. One consulted with the Home Depot chain of stores about carrying the panels. Habitat for Humanity, the international foundation that builds homes for low-income people, was definitely interested because the panels were easy to build with, making them perfect for the skill level of many of its workers. But in each case, the interested parties were unable to obtain the panels. Their interest flagged, and the moment was lost.

By this time, the stockholders were becoming extremely upset. One of the larger investors even considered an unfriendly takeover of the company. This action would have allowed for new management and new policies.

However, no such change occurred. The stockholders began to sell their stock, the price began a precipitous fall, and the rest, as they say, is history.

The Teachings of Failure

What lessons can investors learn from this debacle? Once again, the first lesson is that a great product is by no means a guarantee of success. The second lesson is once more that among the three factors necessary for success—management, financing, and product—good management ranks first. The managers are the ones who have to deal successfully with marketing the product and attracting financing. If they fail, the product will not reach the marketplace.

An investor has to be sure that a skilled, experienced management team is in place. Particularly with young companies, it's vital to ascertain whether a company has grown out of its early stages of development and is ready to handle evolving into a large, successful organization.

INVESTORS AS PROMOTERS

What we are looking for is a small company with excellent management, innovative products, and adequate financing. There are actually quite a few such companies. But we are seeking one more thing: a low stock price.

There are many fine small companies which investors have already discovered. In fact, eager investors may have run the stock price up to an inflated level. We want to find companies with equally fine prospects which have not yet been discovered.

To grow and prosper, a company needs to have backers who are excited about the firm's prospects and will talk about them to anyone who will listen. This is partly the job of the public relations department; the rest is up to you. After you have done your research and firmly believe that a firm is headed for the top, don't hide your excitement. Once the stock is safely in your portfolio, start broadcasting.

Customers with Interest

Real Goods Trading Corporation, a small environmental firm in Northern California, has several stores and a thriving catalog business, selling everything from photo-electric panels to energy-saving appliances to various how-to books. When the time came to expand, the managers considered different ways of raising capital. Issuing stock looked good, but the question arose: who would buy it? The answer was: the loyal catalog customers who strongly supported the company's environmental message.

In 1992, when Real Goods made a limited offer of $1 million of stock at $5 a share, the offer was oversold by $450,000. Encouraged, the company issued 600,000 shares at $6 the next year. The price quickly climbed to

6½; by mid-1994, Real Goods had obtained a listing on the Pacific Stock Exchange and the stock stood at 10½.

The buyers of stock in this tiny firm were doing exactly what I recommend in this book: they were buying into a company they thoroughly understood. As customers, they had watched Real Goods grow and had developed a rapport with the management. They would call to offer advice on new products—or any other pertinent subject.

In addition to supporting the company and its stock, these shareholders were the firm's best advertisers. By no means are all the shareholders customers, but it's likely that any outsider who bought stock in Real Goods heard about it from a customer/shareholder. This is the kind of support which you, as an interested shareholder, can lend to a small company.

But there is a situation of which investors need to beware: the company that is *all* hype. You have probably received fliers in the mail urging you to "investigate the investment possibilities" in some supposedly amazing company. More often than not, the "amazing" company is a struggling mining firm with more claims than cash. Its managers are trying to raise investment capital (yours) so that they can start digging.

Junk mail is generally not a good place to search for promising companies. A certain amount of self-promotion is natural and advantageous, but the kinds of claims made in fancy fliers should arouse your suspicion rather than your interest.

Investors should only choose specific companies with up-to-date information—from newsletters, advisers, company representatives, and other good, current sources. When researching companies through books, even this one, be sure that the information is still valid. The companies portrayed in this chapter were chosen to illustrate certain points, and, as of this writing, a couple of them also look very promising for investors. But books may be read a year or more after publication, enough time for many changes.

CHAPTER 6

USING COMPUTERS

Y ou can get some assistance with your number crunching and even with finding likely companies through the wonders of modern electronics. Information networks and the right software can turn your computer into a tool for investment analysis. Plus, you can trade stocks without leaving your desk.

Tool is the operative word here. Your computer can help you make decisions, but it cannot do everything for you. The investment world has long been searching for formulas that would allow an investor or trader to make money without much thinking: "All you do is wait until the stock has an earnings ratio of lower than 6½ and the market is off its highs by 15 percent relative to the interest rate on the long bond. . . ." A few systems even attempt to predict the markets using such abstruse disciplines as astrology.

Since the advent of the computer, these formulas and systems have proliferated. Some of them work well—for a while. But the markets have a way of confounding attempts to predict their future. A system that worked perfectly for five years may suddenly founder due to an unforeseen event in the world.

When programs and systems are used on a large scale, they can occasionally trigger the opposite of what their operators want. The crash of 1987 was partly a result of program trading by large firms: the programs all said sell at the same time, transforming a market downturn into a total rout.

You simply cannot expect your computer to take the place of your fieldwork, your judgment, or your intuition. Keeping this in mind, there are certainly ways in which computers *can* aid you in making important investment decisions.

DATA RETRIEVAL

The first thing your computer needs to help you with investing is information: a data base. You can get this through a data-retrieval service such as the one provided by the Data Broadcasting Corporation (see Resources). This service provides either up-to-the-minute (real time) stock quotes or, at a much lower cost, just closing quotes. Some data-retrieval systems will also give you quotes on other markets (the futures and options markets, for example), but I'm going to confine my discussion to stocks.

With this information, you can set up a list of the stocks you own and another list of the stocks you're considering buying. This facilitates keeping track of the prices and allows you to see the total value of your portfolio at any given time.

This book emphasizes buying and holding stocks, but should you decide to do some active trading in small stocks, or in any market, having a real-time data-retrieval system is crucial. Prices of volatile stocks can change minute to minute in an active market, and viewing quotes as they change through the day is by far the best way to sell at the highs and buy at the lows.

On the other hand, if you employ a buy-and-hold strategy, you may not need the expensive real-time data and can save money by simply viewing your portfolio at the end of the day. Either way, you will have the data you need to run most investment software.

Discount brokers, such as Charles Schwab, now provide investors with on-line stock trading. In addition, there are a growing number of on-line brokers which charge substantially lower commissions than the traditional

---

Stocks On-line

During the last few years, there has been a proliferation of services offering up-to-the-minute market quotes, information on stocks, on-line trading, chat groups, and advice from the experts. Subscribers to major providers like America Online have access to all of these services, but there are many other Web sites that give investors similar information.

There has also been a proliferation of on-line hype. On bulletin boards and in chat groups, you can find any number of wild claims for the latest penny stock or hot technology company. Claims abound for "sure things" which will "double your money in three months."

If you see a promising recommendation, just run it through the same procedure you would use for any small company that came to your attention. Don't substitute on-line enthusiasm for your own careful research.

discount brokers. If you find yourself doing a lot of buying and selling, you should consider trading on-line. In the future, you may be able to trade directly with other investors. Real Goods, mentioned in Chapter 5, has already pioneered direct trading among its shareholders.

Another advantage to being on-line is that you have access to company Web sites. When you are researching a company, these Web sites are valuable sources of information, providing historical data as well as the latest press releases.

But don't depend only on information from the company. The on-line providers, financial Web sites, and services such as Data Broadcasting also provide detailed analyses of listed firms. In Chapter 2, I recommended the seven-page reports published by Standard & Poor's; Data Broadcasting offers these reports on-line.

In addition, you can find numerous sites where investors "chat" about individual companies. The information to be gleaned from these chat groups is uneven, but often provides insights not found in other places.

SOFTWARE

In the last 10 years, a bewildering array of software has been developed for investors. Some software programs will provide fancy graphs and charts to assist you in the analysis of companies and their stocks. Others will give extensive historical information on any category of stocks (and other investments). Using still other programs, you can set up real or imaginary portfolios and track them as they rise and fall.

There are services that will personalize software to work with your own trading strategies. Perhaps you've observed that stocks in companies with a low price-earnings

(P/E) ratio, a low market-to-book value, and a sharp quarterly increase in income rise higher and faster than other small company stocks. You could then develop a program that would search out companies with those characteristics.

Soon you will have assembled a list of likely companies and can begin your research. Your job is now to discern which of these firms looks the best. You still need to learn about the companies' management, products, niche markets, and so on; you still need to talk to the principals and develop an intuitive feeling for the prospects of any firm in which you're interested. But your software has given you a head start.

Many of the programs available have their own criteria for appraising the thousands of publicly traded companies. If you're interested in this kind of assistance, the publications recommended in this chapter's Resources section will help you choose the best programs, and then you can decide which of these matches your own style of investing.

You may not find any of them helpful. People who are comfortable with computers may find it much easier to do their investing with electronic support. Others tend to get confused by the sheer amount of information available on the financial network. In any case, computers are by no means necessary to the formulation and execution of a successful investment strategy.

Resources

Data Broadcasting Corporation, 1900 S. Norfolk St., San Mateo, CA 94403. (800) 367-4670.

The prices of the information services offered vary widely depending on the urgency of your need for information. Data Broadcasting will send you a complete description of each service with a price list.

It will also send you, upon request, *The Signal Guide to Investment Software,* which describes 130 programs you can use with Data Broadcasting's service, from simple, inexpensive portfolio-management programs to complex analytical software costing thousands of dollars. The catalog gives a half-page of text to explaining the functions and features of each.

Data Broadcasting can even fix you up with a pocket receiver, the QuoTrek, so you can check on your stocks at odd moments during the day.

Computerized Investing, American Association of Individual Investors (AAII), 625 N. Michigan Ave., Chicago, IL 60611. A monthly 24-page newsletter. With membership in AAII ($49/year), a subscription costs $30/year. Without membership, it's $60/year.

If the Data Broadcasting guide to software overwhelms you, this newsletter can help. Included are how-to articles, descriptions and reviews of the latest investment software, and evaluations of data-retrieval systems and financial data bases.

A subscription to *Computerized Investing* includes a free copy of *The Individual Investor's Guide to Computerized Investing*. This regularly updated guide describes hundreds of software programs and financial data bases. The programs cover everything from stocks, bonds, options, and mutual funds to real estate.

AAII is one of the older investor associations. It publishes the monthly *AAII Journal* (except in June and December). It can also put you in touch with one of the many AAII investment clubs, including your local AAII computer-investing group.

CHAPTER 7

INTERNATIONAL INVESTING

"Chinese Economy Shows Greatest Growth." "Southeast Asia: Land of Opportunity." We've been seeing these sorts of headlines for a few years now. But what are the best ways to invest in such faraway places? Is it possible to invest in small companies abroad, or is it too risky? This chapter lays out the different ways of investing abroad, with the advantages and the risks, so you can decide for yourself.

The benefits from putting some of your capital in small foreign companies are readily apparent. You are adding diversity to your portfolio and giving it a greater balance. You may also be able to take advantage of the explosive economic growth in some countries. Although the risk is higher in turbulent economies, well-managed small firms can develop fairly quickly into big companies.

You will also be broadening your knowledge of the investment world and of the world in general. This understanding can only make you a better investor.

MUTUAL FUNDS MAKE SENSE

You can put money into small foreign companies either by buying mutual funds that specialize in small companies from various parts of the world or by getting an international broker and buying shares of specific companies on the foreign stock exchanges. (American Depository Receipts, or ADRs, which make it possible to buy foreign stocks on American exchanges, are issued mainly to large foreign corporations.)

The easiest and safest way of investing in small international firms is through mutual funds. In this instance, it makes sense for a single investor to consider buying mutual funds instead of individual company stocks.

So, if you're interested in expanding your investment horizons, the funds are a good place to start. Some international, small-cap mutual funds are listed at the end of this chapter. You choose the region—Europe, Southeast Asia, Japan—but you are spared the trouble of finding good companies, as this is the job of the fund's managers. That doesn't mean you don't have any homework, however.

It's your job to ascertain where the economies are expanding and where they are not. In 1993, for example, the funds investing in Southeast Asia showed an *average* growth of 50 percent, while funds in many other areas were stuck in a holding pattern.

In addition to checking out the records of the various funds, you will want to learn all you can about the prospects of any country or area you are considering. Are its politics stable? How are its relations with the rest of the world? Is the economy growing? By choosing to invest internationally, you have also chosen the necessity of becoming knowledgeable in world affairs.

Don't depend entirely on the *Wall Street Journal* or *Time* magazine to give you the inside dope on international economies. Successful investing always means going one step farther than the majority of people—learning more than the average investor. This is especially true of international investing.

Some fascinating publications can aid you in this endeavor. Besides two international newsletters, the Resources section lists a few magazines that offer an insider's view of various economies. While subscriptions to these publications are not cheap, the information in them is invaluable. (They are also often available in public libraries.)

The economies of the world interest some people more than others. If you find your interest flagging as you read about the market for tin in Malaysia or the difficulties of the South African economy, perhaps international investing is not for you. Not to worry. Putting money into areas that you're not truly interested in usually turns out to be a mistake. There are more than enough opportunities in the U.S and Canada for small-cap investors.

WORLD-CLASS INVESTING

If, however, you discover that opportunites in the telecommunications industry in Kuala Lumpur seize your interest, you may want to go further than the mutual funds. To purchase stock in international companies, you will need an international broker. The large brokerage houses such as Paine Webber and Merrill Lynch have brokers that can buy on foreign exchanges. The larger discount brokers, like Charles Schwab, can also trade foreign stocks for you.

To find information on individual companies, you should subscribe to one or two of the excellent newsletters listed in Resources. You may not be able to visit China or Argentina, but the newsletter editors make it their business to personally check out companies overseas. (If you *can* visit, so much the better, of course.)

These publications profile companies of all sizes, from large conglomerates to midsize corporations to relatively new, small firms. Just as in this country, the small companies will involve somewhat more risk, along with the chance at much greater profit.

Because many countries are still developing their basic infrastructure, numerous companies based in these countries are small but growing as fast as their national economies. Telecommunications firms have been an excellent example of this. You may find an opportunity to invest in a firm that is the future AT&T of its homeland.

How much should you invest in international small-cap stocks? I recommend a total of no more than 25 percent of your small company portfolio. As promising as the opportunities can seem, there are also potential problems which you need to keep in mind.

Small Treasures

Just as small companies tend to grow faster than large ones, a recent study shows that investing in countries with small stock markets gives substantially better results than investing in countries with large markets. It's noteworthy that the study focused not on emerging markets but on established ones in small countries, such as Denmark, Switzerland, and Belgium, and in the colony of Hong Kong.

Again, just as companies with a small number of stocks can be bid up rapidly, small markets react more strongly to infusions of capital. This makes for increased volatility, but over the long run the smaller markets show a greater increase in value than the larger ones. And greater value in a market usually means that your individual-company stocks will also show a larger increase.

WORLD-CLASS RISKS

International investing certainly carries risks, and they
are compounded when you invest in small companies. In
addition to the risks normally associated with small firms,
you have to consider a number of other possible difficulties.

The Changing Exchange

First among these complications is currency exchange. As
you are doubtless aware, the value of each country's currency rises and falls against other currencies. Many international investors try to predict and take advantage of
these fluctuations by investing in the currency futures
markets. To investors in international stock markets, however, the fluctuations are more of an annoyance than anything else.

When you buy stock in an Australian mining company, you are also, necessarily, speculating on the Australian dollar. In order to purchase the stock, your dollars
have to be changed into Australian dollars—you "buy"
Aussie dollars. But when it comes time to sell the stock
and convert the proceeds back into U.S. currency, the exchange rate will almost certainly be different.

If the Australian dollar has appreciated against the
U.S. dollar, you're in good shape; you'll get more U.S. dollars in the exchange. Should the reverse be true, however,
you will end up with less when you bring the money home.
If the Australian economy should experience serious difficulties, with its currency falling sharply, you could end up
losing on the investment even though your stock went up.

This brings us to a rule about international investing:
Don't put all your money in one country. Sharp declines in
a country's currency can do real damage to your capital.
It's highly unlikely that the U.S. dollar will appreciate
against all other currencies during the next decade. Much

more likely is that it will rise against some, fall against others. This will add to the profits from some of your stocks and subtract from the profits of others. So spread your investments around.

Political Unrest

Currency risk is a hazard no matter where you invest. Political risk, on the other hand, is likely to be a danger in only some countries. If you confine your activities to the Western European democracies and Japan, you will find no more risk than in this country. When you start branching out to other parts of Asia, Africa, Latin America, and Eastern Europe, however, you may find yourself embroiled in wars, revolutions, or, at least, marked changes in economic policies.

Disorder of any kind hurts business. It disrupts commerce, discourages investment, and creates a climate of fear and uncertainty. Prosperity and growth require a certain level of political order to flourish.

Some countries maintain a semblance of order through repressive dictatorships, but investors often find it repugnant to think that their investment dollars might aid such regimes. Despite the rapid growth of the Indonesian economy, for example, the Indonesian government's brutal repression of the population of East Timor repels many investors.

It's important to note that political risk is also currency risk. A country which the investment community sees as inherently unstable is not likely to attract much investment. This will hurt the economy, and the currency will drop in value against other currencies.

Transforming Economies

Economic difficulties present another risk to the international investor. Countries whose economies are on shaky ground are places for only the most risk-tolerant investors.

The nations of Eastern Europe, for example, are struggling to convert their systems to market economies. Nevertheless, the opportunities there look good to some. An educated labor force, government policies that encourage investors, and proximity to the strong economies of Western Europe all make Eastern Europe seem attractive. The Polish stock market, after all, was the fastest growing in the world in 1993 (all 22 stocks!). And because it's just starting out, many of the investment opportunities are in small companies.

The dangers in Eastern Europe are generally more in the realm of economic instability than political unrest (I do not include the countries of the former Soviet Union in this assessment, regrettably). In spite of the changes as people adjust to electing their own governments, most of these countries seem committed to a free-market system.

Yet a serious recession could bring down the small start-ups that look so attractive right now. This is one more instance where the investor has to decide just how much risk he or she wants to bear. Greater risk almost always means the opportunity for greater profits, but if the risk feels overwhelming, the opportunities are not worth the lost sleep.

All these risks translate into a need to do as much research as you can. With the help of the recommended newsletters and journals, you must become an expert on the politics and economies of the countries in which you invest, *before* you invest. A small company may look like a big winner, but if a change in government could be imminent—and hostile to investors—stay out.

CANADA

There is one foreign country where you can invest almost as easily as you can in the United States. I'm speaking, of course, of our good neighbor to the north, Canada. You need to tell your broker whether a stock is traded on the Vancouver Exchange or the Toronto Exchange, but he or she can buy it for you just as quickly as if it were on NASDAQ.

The Canadian exchanges list many interesting small companies. Often a start-up firm in the U.S. will list itself on a northern exchange while it's working at getting on

NASDAQ. Conversely, many Canadian companies can be bought through dealer networks in this country.

The small company investor needs to be aware that hype and inflated claims often surround small companies in Canada. It's a wide open market, so firms with questionable futures may be listed. Many analysts will avoid small Canadian companies for this reason; my position is that investors simply need to take care. I've had excellent results with carefully chosen Canadian firms.

Be aware also of the difference in value between the Canadian dollar and the American dollar. As I write this, the Canadian dollar is worth roughly 70 cents in U.S. currency. When you buy a Canadian stock through an American dealer network, you are buying it in American currency; when you buy on a Canadian exchange, the stock will be listed in Canadian dollars.

The Canadian Outlook

As a market, Canada looks promising these days. The economy is in strong recovery, interest rates are low, and the inflation rate is near zero. Canadian investors and foreign capital are moving into the stock market. Foreign direct investment has grown from C$1.6 billion in 1986 to C$6 billion in 1993.

Canada has a highly skilled labor force, an excellent infrastructure, and low energy rates. By some measures, it has the highest standard of living in the world. The North American Free Trade Agreement (NAFTA) means that Canadian goods and services will have even greater access to the U.S. and Mexican markets.

Several investment newsletters mentioned in this book cover Canadian small stocks. *The ProTrader* (now called *Maedel's Mini-Cap Analyst*) recommends mostly Canadian stocks, while the *New Energy Report* and *OTC Growth Stock Watch* offer a few. *New Energy Report* is listed in Resources, chapter 4, and *Maedel's Mini-Cap Analyst* and *OTC Growth Stock Watch* are in Resources, chapter 8.

Resources

International Small Company Mutual Funds

T. Rowe Price International Discovery

DFA United Kingdom Small Company

DFA Continental Small Company

DFA Japanese Small Company

Scudder Global Small Company

Smallcap World

Templeton Smaller Company Growth

International Publications

The Economist, Subscription Department, P.O. Box 58510, Boulder, CO 80321-8510. $73.50/year.

The Economist is the magazine you read if you want to know what's going on in the economies of the world. Published in England since 1843, it is read by government leaders, academics, and even economists. Despite its elite reputation, this magazine is very readable. Its articles will keep you abreast of the developments you need to follow to be a successful international investor.

Far Eastern Economic Review, 38 W. 38th St., New York, NY 10018-6209. $135/year.

A review of the economies of the Far East, this journal will give you the general knowledge you need to understand the region's market. You need to know not only what's happening in the various countries but also which industries are doing well. This will facilitate your search for promising companies.

Asia Business Journal, Subscription Department, P.O. Box 226, Randolph, MA 02368. 24 issues, $195/year. 12 issues, $110/6 months.

While the two magazines above provide an overall look at the economies of Asia and the world, the *Asia Business Journal* is geared more toward investors. The format is that of a small newspaper. After a few pages of general Asian economic and business news, articles deal with individual countries.

Each country—Australia, Bangladesh, China, Fiji, Hong Kong, India, Indonesia, Japan, North and South Korea, Malaysia, Pakistan, Papua New Guinea, the Philippines, Saudi Arabia, Singapore, Taiwan, Thailand, and Vietnam—has its own page in which business and investment news is discussed. Finally, a few pages are given to the performance of the stock markets in various countries. If you plan to invest in Asia, this periodical is highly recommended.

Newsletters

TAIPAN, 824 E. Baltimore St., Baltimore, MD 21202. Monthly. $79.95/year.

TAIPAN is really half magazine, half investment newsletter. The editors like to write about the technologies and social changes behind the companies they recommend. This usually makes for interesting reading, though I have taken issue with their occasional dark views of the future.

The "January Forecast" issue is a 100-page review of what's happening in countries all over the world. The emphasis is on economics, of course, but the editors just can't help including all sorts of fascinating tidbits about new technologies and social trends.

Although *TAIPAN* covers financial opportunities of all kinds, the bulk of the newsletter deals with stocks, both foreign and American. Many of these are promising small firms; because of the editor's emphasis on new technology, they have come up with some extraordinary companies whose stock has risen as their innovative products have come into favor.

John Dessauer's Investor's World. See Resources, chapter 9. Dessauer will sometimes recommend international small company stocks.

CHAPTER 8

LISTENING TO
THE EXPERTS

I have a real treat for you in this chapter: interviews with four top investment analysts. These analysts all publish newsletters that cover small company stocks, so you can continue to benefit from their expertise, if you wish, by subscribing to their newsletters.

You may be struck by the similarities in how these individuals pick their stocks: for example, they all take plenty of time to study a company's particulars before they will recommend its stock, and they all consider good management to be the prime factor in the success of any firm. You may also notice the differences among them. Each has his own particular style, yet each has achieved a high degree of success.

This is a good place to emphasize that no matter how fine a stock analyst's record is, you need to do some research, too. Your own financial profile of a company and your own gut feeling about the stock are the most important

factors in choosing to invest. The newsletters recommended in this chapter and in the rest of the book are excellent places to start, but they shouldn't take the place of
your own investigations.

MAX BOWSER

The Bowser Report

Started in 1977, the *Bowser Report* is the granddaddy of
the small-stock newsletters. Unlike most analysts, Bowser
has a fixed system for picking stocks which he developed
during the newsletter's first few years. Also unlike most
editor/analysts, Bowser focuses only on stocks selling for
$3 a share or less. While this eliminates some good oppor-
tunities, it keeps the price right for small company investors.

Every month, subscribers receive not only the
newsletter but a two-page supplement that reports the
latest quarterly sales and earnings of the companies previously recommended in the newsletter. Bowser's booklet,
How to Make Money with Stocks $3 a Share or Less, comes
free with a new subscription. This booklet describes the
rating system he uses to pick stocks as well as the buying/
selling techniques for investors.

The *Bowser Report*'s style is pleasantly familiar, as if
the subscribers (and there are many) were all part of one
big investment family. There is usually a chatty interview
on the front page; then, after the recommendation of the
month, much of the letter is given over to reports on companies recommended in earlier issues.

The newsletter has a sister publication, the *Bowser
Directory of Small Stocks,* which follows about 800 small
companies (the number is continually increasing). It is updated monthly and includes data on each firm such as

long-term debt, book value, annual sales and income, shares outstanding, and the Bowser rating for the stock. This directory is meant for investors who want to do their own research. It costs $10 a copy or $89 a year (see Resources for address).

AN INTERVIEW WITH MAX BOWSER

Q. Among the "big three"—management, product, and financials—which do you consider the most important?

A. I'd say that good management's the most important, but it's also the hardest thing to determine. If I know that management is top-notch, I don't even care what business they're in. They could sell horseshoes and make a success of it!

The best way to evaluate management is to look at what they've done with the company so far. Or, if they're new to the company, what have they done in the past? Even if they've been successful in the past, that may not translate into success at the task at hand.

Q. What do you look for in the financials?

A. First, we always insist that a company be profitable. Then we have a rating system of 12 factors, eight of which have to be positive before we'll recommend a stock.

It's important that a small company have a good balance sheet. If they don't have much in the way of assets and they make a wrong decision, then they're down the tubes.

In my experience, the stocks that have done the best are those that have a small number of shares outstanding. For instance, take Three-Five Systems. In 1991, you could have bought that for 2⅝. It eventually went up to around $60. But a big reason for this kind of rise was they only had about 3 million shares outstanding.

Q. How small is small?

A. There are very loose definitions of this—they're all across the landscape. But I think that $100 million market cap or less is a good definition of a small stock.

Q. Is this the size you look for in your stocks?

A. No, we don't. We're price-oriented—and so are most individual investors, because they're spending their own money. Professionals tend to look more at market cap and ignore the price, because they're spending somebody else's money. But I would consider anything under $10 a small stock. In fact, most small company newsletters will recommend stocks up to $10. In our newsletter, we recommend only stocks under $3.

Q. Then you might look at the stock of a large corporation that had fallen on hard times?

A. Sure. In fact, it's been my experience that any low-priced stock on the New York Exchange is more likely to go up sharply than a stock on the OTC or the American Exchange. This is because the listing requirements are much stricter, so that stock almost certainly belongs to a pretty substantial company.

Q. Where do you find your stocks?

A. We start out with the stock tables in the *Investor's Business Daily*. They show the earnings along with the price of the stock. If we see a stock under $3 with good earnings, we'll call up the company and start building a file on them. When we get enough information, we send them through our rating system.

We have another publication, the *Bowser Directory of Small Stocks*. Most of the stocks we research go in this directory. There are over 800 entries now.

Q. Would this be a good place for individual investors to look for companies to do further research on?

A. Yes, the directory is geared for people to do their own research.

Q. What kind of return do you look for? When will you sell a successful stock?

A. Let me illustrate our selling plan. Suppose you buy 200 shares of a stock at $3, and it goes up to $6—it doubles. You now sell 100 shares. This means you've got your money back, ignoring commissions. Now you track the other 100 shares you still own. It'll go up, come down, go up, and come down. Suppose it goes up to $10, but then it comes back 25 percent to $7.50. That's when you sell—at 25 percent off the high.

I've been publishing this newsletter for 18 years, and it's been my experience that most of these low-priced stocks only go up to $6, $7, $8, $9, $10. Then they fall back or stay in that range. This is why it's so important to know when to sell. Too many people fall in love with their stocks; they don't want to sell them because they think they're just going to go up and up and up.

Q. Why do you think most small stocks stop in this price range?

A. Well, there may only be, say, a $300 million total market in a certain industry. This small company might grow until it has $80 million of that total, but if there are a few other competitors, there's a limit to how much it can grow.

Q. How about an unsuccessful pick? At what point will you sell that?

A. You're always going to have those. It's important to sell them when you're convinced that the fundamentals have gone sour. We look more at the fundamentals than we do at any price drop.

Q. You have a personal portfolio of 17 stocks listed in the *Bowser Report*. What has been the yearly average increase of this portfolio?

A. Something better than 30 percent a year. I started that portfolio in 1986. It started off pretty slow but then took off after a couple of years. One thing I've learned over the years is that you have to have a lot of patience.

Q. I'm delighted to hear you say that because it's one of the points I'm trying to get across in my book. Do you have anything else you'd like to say about the *Bowser Report* or investing in general?

A. Keep track of your investments; stay right on top of them. This is one of the strong points of our newsletter: we follow up our recommendations very strongly. The majority of our space is talking about our previous recommendations.

The individual investors who are the most successful are those who keep learning—who constantly increase their knowledge.

BOB ACKER

The Acker Letter

Bob Acker and his wife, Susan, publish *The Acker Letter* from their home. There's no slick advertising here, no fancy graphs or tables, just profiles of small companies which Acker considers undervalued by the market—and undervalued they have been! *The Acker Letter* has the best record of any small-stock newsletter I know.

If you subscribe, you will quickly notice a battle taking place in the pages of this newsletter: Bob Acker versus all the large investors who ignore or sell short the companies he recommends. Whenever one of the recommended stocks sells at a good profit (which is 90 percent of the time), the newsletter headlines will trumpet, "Score one for the good guys/gals!"

Acker sees himself as a champion of the small investor. His goal is not to help someone buy a bigger yacht, he says, but to help a family put their kids through college or to help a couple achieve a secure retirement.

The Acker Letter is entertaining as well as enlightening. As I wrote in the first chapter, small-stock investing is more involving and more fun than putting your money in giant corporations or mutual funds. It's people like Bob Acker who help make it that way.

AN INTERVIEW WITH BOB ACKER

Q. I notice that most of your stocks are under $5 a share when you recommend them. Do you have a rule about that?

A. No, it just works out that way. For one thing, I enjoy writing about the stocks that everybody despises. I like challenging an existing body of knowledge—or lack of knowledge. What fun is there in following a company that has an army of guys in thousand-dollar suits writing about it?

Q. How do you find your companies?

A. I find a lot of my companies by watching where the insider buying is going on. When the market is saying that a stock isn't worth much, but those who are in the best position to know are buying aggressively, then that makes me look very hard.

The other thing I like to look at is the book value of a stock compared to its market price. If the market is ignoring this stock, the book-value can often be higher than the stock price. These book-value stocks are easy to find.

Q. Where do you find them?

A. Sometimes I find them by reading about which industries are most depressed, then looking for the companies in that industry that have been around for a long time and did very well at one time. For example, LTX, which we recommended at 1 5/8 a few years ago, was at one time a big Wall Street darling, a big institutional favorite.

This combination of a company with a good balance sheet and a higher book value than market price is a powerful one, especially when the stock used to trade much higher. Even if we're only right a little more often than we're wrong with these, the payback can be enormous.

Q. Among the three factors—product, management, and financials—which do you look at primarily?

A. I look carefully at the balance sheet and, of course, the product. But it's not enough that the stock looks good financially or that you're impressed with the technology. The people who are running the company have to be the same type of people you would choose as partners. I have to trust them and respect them.

Q. You seem to have a very sharp eye for undervalued stocks.

A. Let me give a textbook example of an undervalued stock. When we found TransNet in January of 1994, the stock was selling for $1 a share, but the book value was around $1.60. They were making good money, they had a terrific balance sheet, and the insiders owned a lot of stock—everything about it was a positive. I called up the president and asked, "What's the catch here? What's hiding in the bushes? There's got to be something wrong!"

But the only thing wrong was that nobody cared about the stock; nobody was paying attention to it. In two months, the price was closing in on $3. We sold half and held onto the rest.

Q. A classic underreported stock.

A. Most of the time, we don't get that lucky. Usually, we recommend a stock, then keep reporting on it and sweat it out for a long time before we make money.

Q. One of the things that interests me about *The Acker Letter* is that you seem to have favorite companies which you will buy and sell over a period of years.

A. Some of these companies, like Research Frontiers, I hope to be with for the rest of my life. We've traded that company so many times and done so well with it that even if it should fail tomorrow, we wouldn't lose.

Q. When will you sell a successful stock? Do you look at the price or the financials?

A. A combination. One thing that immediately pulls the trigger for me is if the stock goes up too fast and seems to be driven by emotions instead of real substance. In a case like that, no matter how much I like the company, we will almost always sell at least a portion of our position.

Another clue for me is the insiders. If I see that the insiders are selling, I get out of the way.

Q. When will you sell an unsuccessful pick?

A. Too late, usually! Everybody has them. They're like dogs lying out in the yard; who knows when they're going to wake up? I actually fault myself for holding onto

stocks too long. I get attached to the companies, to the management. But having said this, I also want to say that some of the biggest successes we've had have come from the stocks we've held the longest. If I had put in sell stops,* we would not own some of our best stuff.

NEIL MAEDEL

Maedel's Mini–Cap Analyst

Neil Maedel started as a clerk on the Vancouver Stock Exchange in 1979. Over the next few years, he worked his way up to senior stock trader with several major securities

---

*A *sell stop* is a standing order with your broker to sell a stock if its price falls to a certain level. This can protect against excessive losses.

firms. He established a newsletter called *The ProTrader* in 1987. During the next three years, he also wrote editorials for the *Vancouver Stockwatch*.

In 1991, when he married and moved to Switzerland, *The ProTrader* ceased publication for two years. From where he and his family live, near Lucerne, Maedel started it up again in March 1993—to the great benefit of its subscribers. From March 1993 to March 1994, the average appreciation of its recommended stocks was 126 percent.

When you talk to Neil Maedel, you hear the language of a professional trader. Nevertheless, the writing in the newsletter, now called *Maedel's Mini–Cap Analyst,* is comprehensible to the average investor. You're getting the best of two worlds here: a professional trader who can make the markets understandable to the nonprofessional.

Each recommended company is profiled in detail, and previous recommendations are updated. Maedel includes a good deal of pertinent information about the markets and the industries the firms are in. Reading this newsletter is an excellent education for the average investor.

AN INTERVIEW WITH NEIL MAEDEL

Q. In choosing a stock, what are the major things you look at?

A. Basically, I always look at management first. There are lots of things that can go wrong, but if you've got a very good management team, they'll react to it and turn it into something worthwhile. And you want them to have a good track record. So management comes first. It's essential.

The second thing is what stage the company is at. Are they at a critical phase that could bring a lot of fast development?

The third thing is that if there is development and things are coming together the way they should be, how is that reflected on a technical basis? Who's buying and who's selling? If insiders are selling, then I'd have to go back to the drawing board.

The good things about a stock should always be confirmed technically—or, at least, not contradicted technically. A sleepy little stock that you're accumulating may not be confirmed by the market; the stock price may be just going sideways and traded very thinly. But before you buy, the stock should be confirmed by the market or by insider buying, or, at the least, be going sideways, not down.

Q. Do you look at insider trading a good deal?

A. I try to get a sense of it. Unfortunately, in the small-cap market, it can be difficult to trace. I like to see management having a significant stake in the company. But the best indication will always be the way it trades: the volatility and the volume. Volatility is usually reduced by bullish insiders: they'll sell the stock when it rises and buy it when it backs off.

If you see a stock rising on big volume, you can bet that a lot of that volume is insider selling, just to hold down the volatility.

Q. Most of your picks are small companies. Do you limit how big you will go?

A. It really depends. For instance, in 1993, we recommended Placer Dome because it looked very good technically, and there were signs that they were upgrading their reserves. In six weeks, it had gone from $25 to $37. For a mammoth blue chip, that's a good trade! So I'm always open-minded and looking for great trades, whether they're very big companies or very small companies. It's just that it comes less often with the big companies.

Q. How many stocks will you hold at one time in the *Mini-Cap Analyst* portfolio?

A. I don't like to get much over 15; it gets too hard to keep track of.

Q. Where do you find your stocks?

A. I'm part of a large network of people, and I'm constantly hearing about things from them. Then I look for the combination of things I mentioned about the companies. Most small venture-capital companies have very weak management, especially in Canada, so this eliminates about 80 or 90 percent of them. Too many of them are the flavor of the month—whatever is easy to promote at that time.

With mining companies, I usually like them to be in production, or almost there, so I can examine their operating skills.

Q. It seems that you look not just at individual stocks but at entire industries.

A. Yes. For instance, I correctly picked the bottom of the oil market in April of 1994. Technically, it looked like it was ready to turn around, and we started recommending some oil stocks.

Q. And you were exactly right. Will you then recommend selling when a market begins to look weak?

A. I don't usually like to defy entire markets, but sometimes in a bear market, I'll recommend companies I think my readers should know about. Take the gold market. In mid-'94, I wasn't bullish on gold. The junior golds

had been hit very hard, right across the board, and were
down 20 percent to 50 percent.

But at the same time, I recommended a few gold
stocks. These were in companies with great management, capable of very fast growth. Small companies like
these are not liquid traders, which means that when gold
turns around, you're just not going to get to buy them at
any reasonable price. They're going to move a lot quicker
than you can, and all you can do is sit there and watch
them go up.

Q. So you have to be positioned in them early.

A. I learned my lesson about this in 1983. Gold looked
like it was due for a big fall, so I sold a promising gold
stock called Breakwater Resources. Gold did drop $100,
but Breakwater developed its Cannon Mine and went up
from $2.25 to $12.50.

The moral is that you can't time things exactly. The
price swings can be extreme, so all we can do is identify
lower premium companies, which have the right combination of management, projects, and money.

Q. What about the money—the financing?

A. The financing isn't always that important when you
buy. Many of the best deals are companies that are un-
derfinanced in the beginning because the market is in a
trough. The financing will usually follow good management in a rising market.

Q. How long will you generally hold a stock, and what
convinces you that it's time to sell?

A. About a year, on the average. But I like to look at
everything individually. Is the management still doing
what they're supposed to be doing? What are the technical underpinnings like, and what kind of financial condi-

tion are they in? And, of course, what kind of results are they getting? If all those things are building and the stock price hasn't reacted yet, I could end up holding a stock for a lot longer than a year.

What usually convinces me to sell is either the stock has become overpriced or it's just a disappointment—there's something I missed about it, something wrong with it, and it's just time to go.

GEOFFREY EITEN

OTC Growth Stock Watch

OTC Growth Stock Watch was established in 1979. Since 1987, the average gain of its recommended stocks has been 24 percent. The editor, Geoffrey Eiten, is well known in the investment world. When he is not contributing articles to financial magazines, he is being quoted in the same publications. He has appeared on the Financial News Network and is quoted on CNBC's "Money Wheel."

Eiten's commentary on the latest developments in the various financial markets appears each month in the newsletter. You will find this well worth reading. He also makes himself available by phone to his subscribers.

After a couple of pages on a new recommendation, the majority of *OTC Growth Stock Watch* is taken up with the latest information on previously recommended stocks. I consider this one of the strongest aspects of the newsletter; the updates are detailed, and specific advice to buy, sell, or hold is given for each stock.

Eiten holds more current stocks in his portfolio than most editors. The last issue I saw had 33. This means that subscribing investors have to pick and choose carefully for themselves from the various recommended stocks. But, of course, I recommend you do that in any case.

AN INTERVIEW WITH GEOFFREY EITEN

Q. What criteria do you use in choosing a stock for *OTC Growth Stock Watch*?

A. The company's got to have a track record of sales and earnings growth of at least 20 percent for the last two years. They have to have a minimum 2-to-1 current ratio* and minimal or no long-term debt.

We look for innovative management; we check them out and see what they've been involved with in the past. We like companies with niche-oriented products or services.

We look for products or services that are recession-proof or at least recession-resistant.

Q. Do you have a limit on market capitalization?

A. We're always under $100 million. And usually, the stocks are anywhere from $5 to $20 a share. Sometimes we recommend stocks over $20.

Q. How many stocks will you hold in the portfolio of *OTC Growth Stock Watch*?

A. Anywhere from 30 to 40, generally.

Q. What kind of return are you looking for? When will you sell a successful stock?

A. In a situation like the newsletter, you may have subscribers getting into the stock at different prices. For instance, we may have initially recommended a stock at $10. Then, suppose it drops down to $5, but we still like the stock and tell people to buy more. So new subscribers might get in at $5.

Current ratio is current assets compared to current liabilities. In this case, the current assets should be twice as much as the total liabilities.

What we tell our subscribers is if they have a 100 percent gain—if the stock doubles from where *they* bought it—to sell half of it. We then recommend that they put the money from that sale into another one of our recommendations, to diversify their portfolio.

Q. What about an unsuccessful stock, one that goes down substantially? When will you sell that?

A. If we don't like the stock anymore, we'll simply get rid of it and take the loss. But if a company has just one bad quarter because of market conditions and we think they can return to their growth rate within six months, we'll hang in there. We may even buy more if we have confidence in the management.

KEY PHRASES

If you send for trial subscriptions or sample copies to these, or other, investment publications, you will receive fliers showing the record of each letter's recommended investments. When you read these ads, you will come across the phrases *average yearly return* and *annualized return*. These terms are distinct, and it's important to know the difference.

The average yearly return is easy to understand. It's exactly what it sounds like: the average of each year's returns from the trading of a newsletter's recommended stocks. If a letter has gains of 8 percent, 25 percent, and 15 percent for three consecutive years, these numbers add up to 48 percent. Divide 48 by 3 and you have an average yearly return of 16 percent.

The annualized return, on the other hand, is calculated with the assumption that you have reinvested any profits from your trading. In other words, it assumes that you are compounding your gains.

Let's look at an annualized return, using the yearly returns from the example above. Suppose you invest $10,000 the first year; at the end of that year, your 8 percent return will leave you with $10,800. You now reinvest the entire $10,800 the second year and get a return of 25 percent. Twenty-five percent of $10,800 is $2,700, which you add to the $10,800 to get $13,500. Finally, reinvesting the $13,500 the third year brings you a gain of 15 percent, or $2,025. This, added to the $13,500, gives you $15,525.

Your three-year gain is $15,525 minus the original $10,000, or $5,525. This is your total return for the three years. Your annualized return is $5,525 divided by three, or $1,841. This can be expressed as a percentage; in this case, the annualized return per year is 18.41 percent.

The annualized return is a higher figure than the average yearly return because each year your gains were compounded, that is, you added them onto your original capital. If you have good returns for a number of years, your annualized return is going to be very high.

Max Bowser's personal portfolio also illustrates the difference between these terms. Bowser's average yearly return from 1986 through 1993 came out to slightly more than 30 percent a year. After eight years of reinvesting all the profits, however, the portfolio grew to almost eight times its original value. This works out to an annualized return of 100 percent a year.

In real life, of course, returns aren't neatly reinvested at the end of each year. You may buy, sell, and reinvest several times during a year. But the overall yearly returns should work out to be approximately the same no matter when you reinvest.

More Potential Puzzlers

Some newsletters emphasize long-term appreciation, with a minimum of buying and selling. Their circulars will use such phrases as *portfolio growth* and *increase in value*. Remember that this increase is only on paper and will go up and down with the value of the stocks in the portfolio.

Average appreciation of stocks in a portfolio can mean that some stocks have been sold while others are still in the portfolio. This means that your profit has been locked in with some stocks but remains subject to the mercies of the markets with the others.

You must understand the terms that appear in the various publications' advertisements in order to get a clear picture of a newsletter's record.

Resources

The Bowser Report, P.O. Box 6278, Newport News, VA 23606. (804) 877-5979. Fax: (804) 595-0622. $48/year.

The Acker Letter, 2718 E. 63rd St., Brooklyn, NY 11234-6814. $150/year. Foreign: $160/year.

Maedel's Mini-Cap Analyst, P.O. Box 28011, Harbour Center, Vancouver, BC, Canada V6B 5L8. (604) 669-8270 U.S. $150/year (but ask about special rates).

OTC Growth Stock Watch, 1040 Great Plain Ave., Needham, MA 02192. (617) 444-6100. $299/year. Foreign subscribers add $15 for airmail. Editor Geoffrey Eiten is offering a special subscription price of $149/year to readers of this book.

CHAPTER 9

THE BALANCED PORTFOLIO

Chapter 3 looked into a balanced portfolio as a means of safeguarding your investment capital. This book promotes small company stocks, but overinvestment in any sector, no matter how promising it may seem, is a prescription for trouble. Instead, spreading your money into several areas gives your portfolio the steadiness it needs to ride out the ups and downs of the financial markets. This chapter will explore the composition of such a balanced portfolio.

BULLS AND BEARS

This country has seen 14 major bear markets in stocks since the end of World War II. Some of the downturns lasted several years, some only a few months. The average decline in value of the stock market as a whole during these times was 25 percent.

Traditionally, the stock market rises until stock prices begin to be based more on speculative value than real worth. Everyone is betting that everyone else will continue to buy and push prices even higher—the famous "greater fool" syndrome. At this point in the market, unfortunately, many small-scale investors decide that stocks look appealing. They are unaware that the professional investors know the market is too high and are either already selling or watching closely for signs of the inevitable downturn.

The small-scale investors' money pushes the market even higher. It is at this stage that some national or world event often throws a scare into investors and makes them decide to sell at least some of their stocks. This event might be the release of some negative statistics on the economy, or it might be a more dramatic incident, like the 1990 war in the Persian Gulf.

In July 1990, many analysts believed that the stock market was overextended. In early August, the prospect of a war with Iraq, which could disrupt the world economy and cause higher oil prices and inflation, gave investors a selling fever, and the stock market plummeted. Because of its inflated prices, the market probably fell farther than it would have otherwise; the prospect of war popped the speculative balloon.

In most such downturns, small companies' stock prices fall farther and faster than those of the larger companies. Collectively, the small-stock prices have always recovered, though some small firms may be damaged or even go under from the economic stresses. This is the reason you need a balanced portfolio. A more serious recession than that of the early 1990s is always a possibility. Such a recession could wreak havoc on many small firms.

But a balanced portfolio will prevent a recession from wreaking havoc on your investment capital. Let's take look at the components of such a portfolio. Then, in the final section, we'll put them all together.

BONDS

Bonds are the best balance for small-cap stocks because they are a completely different kind of investment. Small company stocks can go up like rockets and fall like stones; except during periods of tremendous change in the interest rates, bonds remain relatively stable in price. Small companies usually give investors no income in the form of dividends; bonds give a steady income in the form of interest. Any returns from investing in small firms will come from appreciation in the share price; returns from bonds generally come not from appreciation but from the steady yearly income they provide.

I am speaking, of course, of high-quality government and corporate bonds, not risky vehicles such as junk bonds. If you are heavily invested in small companies, you need low-risk investments to balance the situation. Junk bonds, with returns of 12 to 20 percent and higher, are subject to the same kind of ups and downs as small companies.

Go for the corporate bonds rated AAA and AA by Standard & Poor's. They will give you a couple of points more interest than the U.S. government issues. Buy bonds from several different firms, and plan to hold on to them until they mature. Or purchase shares in a mutual fund specializing in corporates.

The bond market, together with the market value of your bonds, will go up and down with the prevailing regular interest rates. But what you are interested in here is the regular interest income they provide, not their market value. You are seeking safety and a stable income.

BLUE CHIPS

We're still looking for ballast to balance out the high-flying small companies, and giant corporations will help provide it. In times of recession, their stock goes down less and re-vives sooner than that of small firms. You can depend on dividends of 2 to 5 percent, and you should get good ap-preciation in the stock's value if the market performs rea-sonably well.

You have a choice here: you can either research and buy stock in several large firms or you can buy into mu-tual funds that specialize in the blue chips. This depends mainly on whether you want to take the time to research the stocks yourself or leave that up to the fund managers.

In either case, though, make sure that you spread your money around. You need to purchase stock in at least four or five companies or buy into two or three mu-tual funds. Just as with small stocks, putting all your money in one place is a recipe for disaster. Even blue-chip companies are not immune to difficulties and stock depreciation.

UTILITIES

Carefully chosen utility stocks are even safer and more stable than their blue-chip relatives. This is because even in hard times people tend to pay their utility bills. The re-sultant income means that utility stocks go up and down less than other stocks.

It can really be worthwhile to search out the best util-ity companies yourself, rather than opting for the mutual funds that specialize in utilities. What makes utilities spe-cial are their high dividends, but these can vary a great deal, from 4 all the way to 10 percent. While dividend re-turns from the mutuals are usually in the range of 4 to 5 percent, it's possible to find good companies returning two or three points more.

The Resources section of this chapter lists a couple of newsletters that specialize in utilities. The editors are skilled at finding companies that have high dividends as well as excellent prospects for growth.

Also, take note of what these editors have to say about the various groups of utilities, for any industry's outlook changes over time. For example, as I write this in late 1994, the gas companies look much more promising than the electric utilities. Telephone companies also look good right now, but the situation may have altered by the time you read this.

INTERNATIONAL STOCKS

Stocks in international companies provide the kind of diversity a balanced portfolio needs. During the past 30 years, many foreign markets have performed substantially better than U.S. markets. A drop in value in your American holdings may be offset by an increase in your international stocks.

In this instance, buying into the top-performing international mutual funds is often the best way to proceed. You want the funds that invest in large companies, and you want them to be in different areas of the world. You might buy a European fund, a fund specializing in Southeast Asia, and one that invests all over the map. You can investigate to discover which areas look the best, but diversify no matter how attractive one region seems. This is what adds safety to your portfolio.

If you want to try investing in individual stocks overseas, you will need a subscription to one of the fine newsletters recommended in Resources.

This diversified, balanced portfolio is also a buy-and-hold portfolio. As in the case of small companies, the best results from international investments will almost always come from keeping them for a number of years. If a given fund is not performing up to the average in its sector, you might consider selling it when you do your quarterly portfolio review. But, generally, just choose your investments carefully and hold on to them.

If you feel an overwhelming urge to trade and speculate, try doing it with a small percentage of your capital. This will allow you to leave the rest to appreciate at its own rate.

THE BALANCED LOOK

Let's see how these balanced portfolios might look. We're going to examine two; the first is that of a retired couple with a need for steady income, the second that of a younger, single person with a desire for growth and the time to do plenty of research. The contents of your particular portfolio might place it somewhere between these extremes.

Portfolio for Retired Couple

Bonds	30%
Utilities	20%
Blue Chips	20%
International Stocks	10%
Small Companies	10%
Cash	10%

Portfolio for Single Person

Bonds	10%
Utilities	10%
Blue Chips	25%
International Stocks	10%
Small Companies	40%
Cash	5%

In the first portfolio, the bonds and the high-yielding utilities satisfy the need for a steady income. The cash in a savings or money-market account will also generate a little income. In addition, retired people need growth in their portfolios. The overall value of the portfolio needs to rise because inflation will make the income worth less as years go by. And growth can also be used as income: the couple can sell assets that have appreciated in value.

These days, many newly retired couples have 25 or 30 years to look forward to, so growth in assets becomes even more important. Hence the majority of this couple's assets are in stocks, and small companies are an important component of the portfolio.

The individual who owns the second portfolio has little need for extra income and wants to focus on growth. He has time to research small firms, and because of this, he feels justified in having 40 percent of his capital in this category. For a person unwilling or unable to do the necessary research, this would be an excessive amount.

This portfolio is going to fluctuate in value a good deal more than that of the retired couple. But if history is any guide, the overall direction will be up, and up substantially, if this investor has done his homework.

Resources

Utility Forecaster, P.O. Box 1462, Alexandria, VA 22313-9888. (800) 892-3737. $87/year. $174/two years.

During the 1980s, utility stocks outperformed industrials by almost 50 percent. This was partly due to the utilities' high dividends (which were reinvested, in these statistics), but was also due to the excellent growth of the stocks. If you need the income, you can have the dividends paid directly to you instead of reinvested; well-chosen stocks can yield 5 to 9 percent. The letter explains both how to obtain the dividends directly and how to have them reinvested in the companies' stocks.

Since it started in 1989, *Utility Forecaster* has earned an annualized return of more than 20 percent for its subscribers. The editor has a buy-and-hold strategy that fits in well with a balanced portfolio.

Young's Intelligence Report, Philips Publishing, 7811 Montrose Rd., Potomac, MD 20854. (800) 777-5005. $177/year (but ask about special rates).

Young is a conservative investor. His specialties are bonds, utilities, high-yielding blue chips, and certain conservative mutual funds. Aiming for a return of 11.5 percent, he has accomplished that and better for his subscribers. Young's emphasis is on safety—he calls his recommended portfolio "bulletproof"— and this emphasis will foster the balance you want for your own portfolio.

John Dessauer's Investor's World, Philips Publishing, 7811 Montrose Rd., Potomac, MD 20854. (800) 777-5005. $99/year. $179/two years.

John Dessauer has been recommending international stocks and mutual funds for quite a while. A few small companies appear in *Investor's World,* but mostly you will find larger blue chips suitable for the international section of your portfolio.

You will also find some excellent analysis of why certain countries or regions are better places to invest at certain times. Dessauer will often recommend closed-end mutual funds that cover these countries. (*Closed-end* mutual funds trade on the exchanges like individual stocks. Otherwise, they have the same advantages of diversification and professional management as the more common open-end mutual funds.)

Dessauer travels a good deal, visiting many of the firms he recommends. He endorses a few solid American stocks as well.

The U.S. Investment Report, Quickel International Corporation, 65 Chapel Road, New Hope, PA 18938. (215) 862-1313. $275/year. Foreign: $325/year. 24 issues a year.

Here is the best large-company newsletter I have found. The editor, Stephen Quickel, recommends a number of stocks, but what catches one's eye are the records of the portfolios in the newsletter. Since January of 1987, $100,000 invested in the growth leaders portfolio would have grown to $8,860,000 by

January of 1998. In the emerging growth portfolio, started on July 1, 1995, $100,000 would have grown to $270,000 by January of 1998.

These are records worthy of small company stocks, but the recommended firms are generally substantial corporations. This newsletter is a great addition to the resources necessary to build a balanced portfolio.

CHAPTER 10

FINANCIAL STATEMENTS

During the 1970s, an advertising agency took on the task of selling an obscure South American wine. The executive in charge concocted a story about a mythical bird that appeared on the wine's label. This fabrication, repeated on radio and in print, caught the public's imagination and sales of the wine soared—for a while. Unfortunately, few people bought a second bottle; the wine was of inferior quality, thin and sour-tasting.

The ad executive simply shrugged and stated the obvious: You can sell almost anything once with clever advertising. But continued sales depend on quality.

This truth applies to small companies. A company can look like a winner: the product is in demand, the balance sheets look sound, and the management seems competent and confident. Yet keep in mind the possibility that all this is only a successful facade. The company has every interest in appearing strong because it wants to keep investors interested. Strong investor interest sustains a high stock price, allowing the company to issue more stock without diluting the share price. This added capital facilitates faster growth.

It's up to you to look past the glossy face a company shows to the world. The best way is to inspect the financial statements with the cold eye of an accountant. Is the company showing a profit? Is the profit increasing each quarter, and if not, why not? If it is not showing a profit, is it moving in the direction of profitability? Is the amount of debt manageable or increasing too rapidly?

These questions and many more can be answered by perusing the balance sheets and the income statements. Infrequently, dishonest managers will feed inflated or distorted numbers to their accountants, but generally you're looking at the real story.

When you become interested in a company, you need to request certain financial statements from it. These are the documents the firm must file with the Securities and Exchange Commission (SEC). Ask for the most recent 10K (annual report) and the one from the previous year; ask also for the latest 10Q (quarterly report).

These reports include thorough descriptions of the company's business, the yearly or quarterly operations, the managers, and so on. While scanning these pages can be useful, don't feel that you have to read everything. The company's brochures and reports from financial analysts will summarize this information. Save your energy for the balance sheets and income statements, which definitely require a thorough reading.

In the case of small start-ups, you will often find a statement in the 10K report that reads: "There is substantial doubt about the company's ability to continue as a going concern." Although this sounds bad, it should not be cause for alarm. This is accountants' language for an investment with some risk. Direct your attention instead to the balance sheet and the income statement; if these are showing improvement from year to year, quarter to quarter, there is every reason to believe that the company will survive.

BALANCE SHEETS

The balance sheet is like a snapshot of a company's financial position at a given date. This statement is always done on the last day of the corporation's fiscal year. In addition, the 10K report will usually show the previous year's balance sheet, so that you can see how the company has performed during the last two years.

A company's fiscal year may not coincide with the calendar year. A fiscal year can end on the last day of any month, though this date usually coincides with the end of a quarter—March 31, June 30, September 30, or December 31.

In addition, corporations put out balance sheets as part of the 10Qs they prepare for the SEC. In these quarterly reports, the position of the company is compared with its position in the same quarter of the previous year (not in the quarter that preceded the present one).

A balance sheet portrays all the assets and liabilities of a company. These are presented sometimes side by side, or sometimes one after the other on the same page, as shown on page 118. Although you will notice different formats from different companies, there are certain rules that are always followed. For example, the total number of assets must equal the total liabilities.

Let's look at the balance sheet of a mythical corporation. (Any resemblance between this balance sheet and that of any real corporation, living or dead, is probably unavoidable, but inadvertent.)

A SAMPLE BALANCE SHEET

Assets

	1994	1993
1. Current Assets		
Cash	$ 775,000	$ 640,000
Marketable Securities	340,000	520,000
Accounts Receivable	920,000	530,000
(doubtful accounts: $25,000)		
Inventory	555,000	245,000
Total Current Assets	$ 2,590,000	$ 1,935,000
2. Fixed Assets		
Plant and Equipment	$ 4,320,000	$ 4,180,000
Furniture and Fixtures	320,000	280,000
License, Technology, and		
Know-how	245,000	280,000
Total Fixed Assets	$ 4,885,000	$ 4,740,000
3. Other Assets		
Goodwill	$ 140,000	$ 165,000
Total Assets	$ 7,615,000	$ 6,840,000

Liabilities

	1994	1993
4. Current Liabilities		
Accounts Payable	$ 1,230,000	$ 885,000
Notes Payable	180,000	160,000
Interest Payable	10,000	5,000
Taxes Payable	55,000	45,000
Total Current Liabilities	$ 1,475,000	$ 1,095,000
5. Long-term Liabilities		
10% Mortgage Bonds		
(due 1998)	$ 620,000	$ 650,000
6. Shareholders' Equity		
5% Preferred Stock	$ 360,000	$ 360,000
Common Stock	$ 5,160,000	$ 4,735,000
Total Shareholders'		
Equity	$ 5,490,000	$ 5,095,000
Total Liabilities	$ 7,615,000	$ 6,840,000

Explanation of Balance Sheet

Current Assets (1).   These include cash on hand and all other assets that can be converted into cash in less than a year, such as government bonds or stock in other companies. A company expects to collect all its accounts receivable and sell its present inventory of goods in less than a year.

On this particular balance sheet, notice the large increases in accounts receivable and inventory from 1993 to 1994. This should set off alarms in your head. Check the company's income statement (on pages 121–122); in this case, there was not a great increase in gross sales. So why aren't customers paying? And why is there much more unsold product in 1994 than in 1993?

There could be a problem with the product, or because of lessened demand, the company could be giving extremely lenient terms to its customers. These increases require further explanation, so call up the company.

Fixed Assets (2).   Also called long-term assets, these include such things as buildings and machinery. They are not intended for sale, but are necessary for the operation of the business.

Other Assets (3).   Such intangibles as goodwill are usually included in the list of assets. Like other assets, goodwill is depreciated for tax purposes each year, hence the difference in value from 1993 to 1994.

The rest of the changes from 1993 to 1994 are not unusual. They could result from either depreciation or normal fluctuations.

Current Liabilities (4).   These liabilities are due and payable within one year. The only unusual change from year to year for this company is in the accounts payable. In the case of such an increase, you need to check the income statement to see whether there is a corresponding increase in net income. If there is, then the company is simply expanding and the accounts payable would logically have increased. If the net income is steady or down, on the other hand, then you need to be concerned about this increase.

Long-term Liabilities (5).   Also known as funded debt, this is any debt security with a due date of more than one year from the date of the balance sheet. In this case, the only funded debt security is the 10-percent mortgage bonds. Most small companies issue a great deal more stock than bonds because it's not necessary to pay a dividend on the stock. The bonds, on the other hand, require payments every six months.

The amount of debt held by this company is not excessive. When the long-term debt begins to approach 40 to 50 percent of total assets, you should start getting seriously concerned. The money needed to pay off the debt will cut into profits as well as research and development—the money the firm needs to grow.

But as long as the debt is not excessive, an increase in long-term debt during a given year is not necessarily a bad sign. Growing firms need funding to grow further, and the fact that lenders think they're a good risk can be a positive sign.

Shareholders' Equity (6).   This is the preferred and common stock issued by the company. The current price of the stock is multiplied times the number of shares outstanding to get these figures. Notice that, unlike the common stock, the preferred stock has a stated dividend that must be paid, in this case 5 percent of par value $100 (the usual value of most preferred stock when issued), or $5 per share.

Working Capital.   By subtracting the total current liabilities from the total current assets, we get an important figure, that of working capital. In 1993, this figure was $840,000, in 1994, $1,115,000. This is a good trend; a growing company should show a healthy increase each year. Working capital is the money a company uses to run its day-to-day operations. The more working capital a company has, the more it is able to expand its volume and take advantage of opportunities.

INCOME STATEMENTS

The income statement is also known as the *profit and loss statement* or the *statement of operations.* It covers profit or loss and expenses for the past year. The comparison between the figures for the present year and the previous one is critical to the prospective investor for obvious reasons. As for one important figure, if the net profit is on the upswing, the firm will look more appealing to the investor.

Here is the income statement for the same fictitious company we've been examining.

A SAMPLE INCOME STATEMENT

	1994	1993
1. Gross Sales	$ 6,835,000	$ 5,450,000
Cost of Goods Sold	3,290,000	3,960,000
Gross Profit	$ 3,545,000	1,490,000
2. Operating Expenses		
Sales, General, and		
Administrative	$ 1,480,000	$ 1,670,000
Research and Development	640,000	435,000
Amortization	230,000	235,000
Interest on Bonds	45,000	45,000
Total Operating Expenses	$ 2,395,000	2,385,000
Operating Income before Taxes	$ 1,150,000	$ (895,000)*
Taxes	55,000	25,000

(continued)

3. **Net Income (Loss)**	$ 1,095,000	$ (920,000)
Preferred Stock Dividend	45,000	45,000
Available Earnings	$ 1,050,000	$ (965,000)
4. **Earnings per Share**	$ 0.14	$ (0.13)
Number of Common Shares		
Outstanding	7,500,000	7,500,000

* Parentheses indicate that the amount is a loss rather than a profit.

Explanation of Income Statement

Gross Sales (1).   The gross sales of this company are up substantially, and the cost of goods sold is down. As a result, the gross profit more than doubled from 1993 to 1994.

Operating Expenses (2).   Here is more good news. While the total operating expenses are almost the same from year to year, there are nonetheless several positive developments in this category. First, the cost of sales has gone down, and, second, the amount spent on research and development has gone up. The latter figure, which is extremely important in a small, growing company, is the reason you should not expect dividends from a small firm: it needs to put all the money it can into improving the product.

Amortization is the gradual devaluation of assets. As buildings, machinery, and office equipment grow older, their value lessens. This yearly depreciation is subtracted from yearly income.

Net Income (3).   The positive change in net income from 1993 to 1994 is dramatic. If you are thinking of investing in a company, such a change would be one of the main factors to consider.

Earnings per Share (4).   Available earnings means "available earnings to the common stock." If the company paid a dividend, it would come out of this figure. Notice that the earnings per share is figured using the available earnings, not the net income. The preferred dividend has to be paid before any earnings are available to the common stock.

Because this is a small firm, probably no dividends will be paid to the common stock. The money will be used instead to finance further growth.

Price-Earnings Ratio

We can arrive at several important numbers by scanning the balance sheet and the income statement. The first one is the price-earnings ratio (P/E ratio). The equation is: P/E Ratio = Market Price ÷ Earnings per Share.

You will find the earnings per share near the bottom of the income statement; in this case, they are $0.14 a share. Next, look up the market price of the stock in the newspaper; let's say it's $1.25 a share. Dividing 1.25 by .14 gives us a P/E ratio of about 9. This is a low P/E ratio compared to the big corporations on the S&P 500 list. They generally have P/E's of between 10 and 25 (since 1945, the average P/E of the S&P 500 has been 14). Most newspapers will list the earnings of stocks and some will calculate the P/E ratio for you, based on the price of the stock for that day.

Analysts like to use P/E ratios to decide whether a stock is undervalued, that is, whether the share price is low in relation to the earnings. This can be useful when studying the giant corporations because their earnings and share prices tend to be fairly stable.

With small companies, however, the P/E is less meaningful because their earnings fluctuate markedly from quarter to quarter. Often they post negative earnings. The share prices also tend to rise and fall dramatically for reasons that may have nothing to do with earnings or other fundamentals.

Therefore, it's not a good idea to decide whether or not to invest in a small company on the basis of its P/E at any given time. Where the P/E becomes useful is in looking at trends. A P/E that is going down steadily is a very positive factor for prospective investors. A big upturn in the ratio may signal a drop in earnings or a large increase in the price per share of the outstanding stock, or both. This increase might mean that overenthusiastic investors have run the price of the stock up to an unfounded value, and investors should generally see it as a signal to defer buying until the price comes down.

Book Value

Another important figure is the book value of the stock, also known as *book value to the common*. This is a ratio of the company's net worth to the number of outstanding shares. It can be calculated: Book Value = Net Worth ÷ Number of Common Shares Outstanding. The stock's book value is what it would be worth if the company had to go out of business and liquidate all its assets.

We can figure the book value of the stock of our imaginary company by referring to the balance sheet and income statement. Net worth is calculated by first subtracting the current and long-term liabilities from the total assets. In this case, the total assets are $7,615,000 and the liabilities add up to $2,095,000. This gives us a figure of $5,520,000.

Now, since the value we want is only in relation to the common stock, we need to subtract the value of the preferred stock, which in this case is $360,000. We also subtract the intangible assets such as goodwill, valued here at $140,000. The final figure for net worth, then, is $5,020,000.

On the income statement, we see that there are 7,500,000 common shares outstanding. Dividing this figure into $5,020,000 gives us .68. This is the book value of the stock: $0.68 per share.

The book value is useful because it can be compared to the market price of the stock. Usually, the market price will be substantially more than the book value. On the rare occasions when the stock's book value is greater than its market price, you should sit up and take notice. You have found a stock that is greatly undervalued by the market.

Further research is needed, of course. You need to learn why investors are disregarding this company. Is it in trouble, or is it actually in excellent shape and simply ignored by the investment community? In the latter case, you may have a buy on your hands.

FINANCIAL PROFILES

Using the data from the balance sheet and income statement, you can set up a financial profile of a company. The model for this appears on page 126, so that you can copy it and use it for any firm in which you're interested. Once you fill in the blanks, you will have before you the most important financial information about the company.

If the working capital is decreasing year by year, if the long-term debt is more than 50 percent of total assets, if the sales are increasing but the net earnings are declining, you will know that it's probably time to look elsewhere. If, on the other hand, working capital and net earnings are steadily increasing and the P/E ratio is going down, you will want to continue your investigation of this company.

With a little experience, you will be able to glance at a financial profile and decide almost immediately whether the firm bears further research.

FINANCIAL PROFILE

Company_____

Last Date of Financial Year_____

	199_	199_	199_
Net Sales	_____	_____	_____
Net Earnings for the year	_____	_____	_____
Net Earnings for the most recent quarter	_____	_____	_____
Total Assets	_____	_____	_____
Current and Long-term Liabilities	_____	_____	_____
Net Worth	_____	_____	_____
Working Capital	_____	_____	_____
Long-term Debt	_____	_____	_____
Outstanding Shares	_____	_____	_____
Earnings per Share for the year	_____	_____	_____
P/E Ratio	_____	_____	_____
Book Value	_____	_____	_____
Share Price/high and low	_____	_____	_____
Present Share Price	_____	_____	_____

Let's look at the financial profiles of two companies. One is not doing well, while the other appears to be in fine shape.

FINANCIAL PROFILE

Company_____ A _____

Last Date of Financial Year   March 31 _____

	1997	1996	1995
	In thousands (add 000)		
Net Sales	$ 7,563	$ 7,890	$ 6,567
Net Earnings/year	1,783	2,186	(1,259)
Net Earnings for the most recent quarter	266	475	(364)
Total Assets	19,673	19,439	16,300
Current and Long-term Liabilities	9,023	7,656	7,197
Working Capital	2,960	4,817	1,879
Long-term Debt	685	345	215
Outstanding Shares	6,550	4,185	3,892
Earnings per Share/year	.27	.52	(.32)
P/E Ratio	12	9.5	NA
Book Value	1.62	2.81	2.33
Share Price/high and low	4½ 2½	7¾ 3	3½ 1⅝
Present Share Price	3¼		

ANALYSIS OF COMPANY A

Company A is having some troubles. After a banner year in 1996, not only have net sales fallen off, but earnings for fiscal 1997 and for the latest quarter have dropped. Both liabilities and long-term debt are up, and the company has issued almost 2½ million more shares of common stock. This has lowered the earnings per share substantially and raised the P/E ratio.

Issuing so many new shares may also have contributed to the stock's fall in price. The value of the outstanding shares can be watered down by the introduction of a large number of new shares. Unless the net worth is increasing, the stock's book value is pushed way down. This has happened here.

If you are thinking of buying a firm with a financial profile like company A, forget it. Now is not the time.

Unless some other extremely exciting things are happening, you missed the boat on this one. The time to buy would have been sometime in 1995, when the firm was just moving into profitability.

If you are holding company A, having bought it when the price was up to $6 in 1996, don't despair just yet. Call up the company's managers to find out what their plans are for the future. The figures for 1997 are not down very much from 1996, and they are still much better than they were in 1995.

The fall in the stock price may be a combination of investor disappointment at the leveling off of earnings and the watering down of the stock with too many new shares. If earnings start to rise again, the stock probably will, too. Continue to watch the quarterly reports and think positive thoughts.

FINANCIAL PROFILE

Company_____ B_____

Last Date of Financial Year_____ December 31_____

	1997	1996	1995
	In thousands (add 000)		
Net Sales	$10,672	$ 7,895	$12,319
Net Earnings/year	4,617	2,856	5,528
Net Earnings/most recent quarter	1,563	287	2,894
Total Assets	25,167	23,532	22,418
Current and Long-term Liabilities	8,496	7,831	7,485
Working Capital	5,269	4,138	5,174
Long-term Debt	3,743	3,692	2,289
Outstanding Shares	4,450	4,223	4,185
Earnings per Share/year	1.03	.67	1.32
P/E Ratio	2	6.5	9.5
Book Value	3.74	3.7	3.5
Share Price/high and low	3$7/8$ 1$1/2$	10$3/8$ 2$5/8$	15 5$1/2$
Present Share Price	2$1/4$		

ANALYSIS OF COMPANY B

Buy! If you spot a company like this, run, do not walk, to the nearest telephone to call your broker. Do this before other investors notice that the book value is one-and-a-half times higher than the market price, or that the yearly and quarterly earnings have jumped significantly since 1996, or that the P/E ratio is 2.

Financial profiles often tell stories. From this one, we can infer that the firm probably had an excellent year in 1995, prompting an impressive rise in the stock. Disaster struck in 1996: almost everything on the income statement took a big dip, which caused investors to sell off the stock as quickly as they had bought it. By the end of 1997, the stock was off its lows but remained down at 2 1/4.

What most investors didn't notice, however, was that despite the dips in sales and earnings, the company maintained a sound financial profile even in 1996. And, by the end of 1997, this profile was astounding. Naturally, you still have to check out other factors, such as the management and the product line, and you need to find answers to certain questions: What caused the '96 downturn? Could this happen again?

But if everything checks out, you have a probable winner on your hands. Stocks like this don't come around every day.

The great advantage to doing a standard financial profile on all the companies you research is that you can tell at a glance whether the company is worth learning more about. You will find that the income statements and balance sheets look different from business to business because various formats are used. But the information is usually all there. The profile allows you to put the most important financial information in a format to which you're accustomed.

Chapter 11

Timing Your Transactions

When to Buy

By the time you are ready to buy stock, you should have a nice, fat file on the company. You will have made up a financial profile, read as many reports as you could get, talked to the information officer, and decided whether the management, products, and niche market look promising. Moreover, you should have a feel for the company.

I urge you to trust your intuition and to delay buying until your gut feeling is positive. The best choice in any situation is made through an internal consensus; trusting only your intellect, or only your feelings, severely limits your ability to arrive at the best decision.

If you basically feel good about a firm's prospects but have some lingering doubts, remember that you can buy only a small amount of stock. This keeps you in touch with the company but limits your exposure to risk. If the situation starts to look more enticing, you can always add to your position.

WHEN TO SELL

Deciding when to sell is usually more difficult than deciding when to buy. A stock that has risen substantially presents you with the question of whether it will go yet higher. A stock that has fallen makes you wonder if it will ever rise.

Surprise!

Various studies have shown that a surprise in the earnings report for any given quarter can signal an upcoming rise or fall in a company's stock during the following year. A report that is substantially better than expected means the stock is more likely to rise; a negative report means the stock is likely to fall.

It may seem obvious that a positive report may send a stock higher, and that a negative report may do the opposite, but the statistics show not just an immediate upturn but a rise over the next six months to a year. This is important because it indicates that you don't have to rush out and buy a stock on the basis of a good earnings report. You still have time to consider the other factors in your decision.

Conversely, a sharp downturn in earnings during a quarter should cause you to take a hard look at any company whose stock you own. Unless other factors remain positive, this surprise might signal that it's time to sell.

The best strategy is to continue following the company as if you were going to buy its stock. If the stock has risen sharply, look at the financial reports. What is the new P/E ratio? If the earnings have gone up in tandem with the price rise—or have outstripped the rise—the company may still be worth keeping.

If, on the other hand, the company has become the darling of the investment community and the stock has risen to unrealistic heights (that is, a price unsupported by a large rise in earnings), then it's probably time to sell. These "darlings" have a way of suddenly falling out of favor with investors—often too suddenly for you to sell at a good price.

When you were doing the original research on the company whose stock you are now considering selling, one of the figures you gathered was the total market for the industry this firm is in. If earnings have leveled off, your company may have reached a position of stasis with its competitors. In this case, further growth is unlikely.

One option is to sell a portion of your stock. If you bought 1,000 shares, sell 500 and hold on to the rest for possible greater gains. Max Bowser of the *Bowser Report* (see chapter 8) recommends selling half of one's shares after a stock doubles. Then he follows the other half to a new high, selling when the stock has fallen 25 percent from that high.

Navigating the Bumps

Anyone who owns small company stocks knows that they will experience a lot of ups and downs. Generally, the right attitude is to ignore the minor fluctuations.

But if a stock falls substantially and then does not move for a few months, you need to take a fresh look at the company, just as if you were considering buying. Indeed, this might be exactly what you should do—buy! If the firm's fundamentals still look good—or even better than when you bought—then the drop in price may have more to do with fickle investors than with the company's actual prospects. Eventually, the firm will be recognized for the diamond that it is. In this case, you may want to buy additional stock and lower your cost basis.

The Acker Letter (see chapter 8) specializes in companies like this. Bob Acker rails against the short sellers and institutional investors who ignore these hidden gems, and exhorts his readers to look past the stock price to the fundamentals. And he has been proven right much more often than wrong.

Nevertheless, if the financials continue to look bad for two or three quarters and no improvement is in sight, you may want to sell and put your money into a company that shows more promise. This should be a judgment call rather than a pat decision based solely on poor financials. You may still have reason to believe that the product and management are winners and can pull the firm out of its doldrums. Again, you're going to have to trust your gut feeling as well as your intellect.

The important thing when you have a loser is not to kick yourself around the room or swear off small-stock investing forever. Even the best analysts occasionally pick losers; it's part of the game.

Striking Gold

Very occasionally, if you're lucky, you may find a company which you want to keep indefinitely. Some firms continue to show improved earnings year after year. They may even outgrow their small company status and start paying dividends. The stock splits; then, in a few years, it rises to where it was before the split, splits again, and pays a double dividend. . . . Why sell? You probably bought it when it was under $10 a share. You're sitting pretty.

William Martindale, a prominent manager of small-cap investments, tells of buying 50 shares of a small firm called Unifi in 1970, at $4 a share. Today, with many stock splits over the years, the 50 shares have grown to 1,200 and the price of the stock is $35 a share.

He held on to Unifi. One he didn't hold on to was Radio Shack. In 1966, he bought $1,000 worth of stock in Radio Shack. He sold it a year later for a slight profit. Had he held it until 1982, the $1,000 would have grown to $500,000—another argument for the buy-and-hold method.

Conclusion

The price of a stock may rise for many reasons. With small companies, these reasons often have to do with inflated investor expectations. You need to look past the enthusiasm and carefully peruse the balance sheets and income statements. As a long-term investor, your decisions should be based on fundamentals rather than on hopes and dreams. These fundamentals, combined with good products and creative management, are the power that will make a company grow over the years.

Having said this, however, I want to emphasize that sometimes you need to look past the balance sheets. The financial pictures of quite a few start-up companies don't look rosy on paper, but the product and the management may look terrific. You will have to base your final decision on your overall sense of the company and its prospects.

Remember, you don't have to bet the farm. You can start out small and invest more later, as the fundamentals improve.

FEAR OF FLYING

When someone is afraid of taking a flight on a commercial airliner, a friend or relative will inevitably refer to the statistics on flying safety, saying: "You're safer than you are riding in a car." Statistically speaking, this person is correct. Considering the number of flights on any given day and the number of things that could go wrong, the airlines have an excellent safety record.

The figures rarely reassure fearful fliers, however. They argue that if something goes wrong in an automobile, they can pull over and call for road service. And, if an accident should happen while they're driving, they are likely to survive. But a mechanical difficulty or collision in the air, they protest, is a much more serious matter.

This is unarguably true. Traveling thousands of feet above the ground is inherently more dangerous than traveling on the ground. Yet the airlines counter this difference by insisting on stringent safety features: frequent and thorough inspections of the aircraft, highly trained personnel both in the craft and on the ground, and a ground control system with the best personnel and technology available.

The great advantages to flying make all this effort worthwhile. Reaching a distant city or country in a few hours, as opposed to days or weeks by car or train, is a powerful incentive to fly.

HIGH-VELOCITY INVESTING

The analogy to the stock market is an obvious one. High-speed aircraft require special care. If you're trying to reach your financial goals more quickly by buying small company stocks, then it's worthwhile to exercise more care in choosing your investments.

Chapter 3 explained the four ways of making your small-cap investments secure. Paying attention to these strategies—knowledge, diversity, buying and holding, and portfolio balance—takes more time than buying a group of mutual funds, but this attention will result in both greater safety and greater rewards.

Mutual funds and blue chips are the ground travel of the investment world; small company stocks are the airplanes. And, occasionally, if you do your research well, you will find yourself riding a rocket.

HIGH ADVENTURE

There are many people whose fear of flying keeps them away from small company stocks. Others simply don't want to spend time on the necessary research. This is fine; don't push them. Their reluctance leaves the field open to those of us who enjoy the interest, the diversity, and the fun of small company investing. Fewer people in a field means greater opportunities.

I hope you will take advantage of the excellent newsletters profiled in this book—or find your own. Having the pros on your side puts you several giant steps ahead of the game. You still need to do your own research, but the head start can be invaluable. My hope is that the material in this book will help you to accomplish your research quickly and easily.

Moreover, I hope the investment strategies I've described bring you many rewards, both tangible and intangible. You are one of the adventurers of the investment world. Good luck!

DECIMAL EQUIVALENTS

In the stock listings in Canadian newspapers you will see stocks selling for under $5.00 a share listed in decimals. For example:

	High	Low	Close
AZCO Mining	$3.35	3.15	3.20

This makes eminent good sense; our currency is based on the decimal system, stocks are purchased in dollars and cents, and electronic calculators operate with the decimal system. So why do American stock dealers still insist on trading with fractions instead of decimals? I expect it has more to do with tradition than with common sense.

This insistence on fractions makes the following table necessary when buying and selling small stocks. In the newspapers, you are likely to see listings such as this one:

	High	Low	Close
Current Technologies	1/4	5/32	7/32

The table shows the closing price of $7/32$ to be .21875 in decimal terms, or 21.875 cents. If you bought 1,000 shares of Current Technologies at $7/32$, you would multiply 1,000 times .21875 = $218.75. This would be what you would pay for the stock, plus commission.

Note that the high price of the day, $1/4$, could also be listed as $8/32$. Printing it as $8/32$ would make it easier for the reader to compare the high, low, and close prices, but the compilers of the stock tables insist on reducing the fraction to $1/4$. It's up to the reader to note that in the table below, $1/4$ is the next listing after $7/32$.

The table is listed in $1/32$ increments, but just as in the stock tables, the fractions are reduced to their lowest common denominators. Five-sixteenths therefore is actually $10/32$, and $1/2$ is $16/32$.

Someday, perhaps, decimal common sense will prevail, but don't hold your breath waiting.

A1. DECIMAL EQUIVALENTS

$1/32$ — .03125		$17/32$ — .53125	
$1/16$ — .0625		$9/16$ — .5625	
$3/32$ — .09375		$19/32$ — .59375	
$1/8$ — .125		$5/8$ — .625	
$5/32$ — .15625		$21/32$ — .65625	
$3/16$ — .1875		$11/16$ — .6875	
$7/32$ — .21875		$23/32$ — .71875	
$1/4$ — .25		$3/4$ — .75	
$9/32$ — .28125		$25/32$ — .78125	
$5/16$ — .3125		$13/16$ — .8125	
$11/32$ — .34375		$27/32$ — .84375	
$3/8$ — .375		$7/8$ — .875	
$13/32$ — .40625		$29/32$ — .90625	
$7/16$ — .4375		$15/16$ — .9375	
$15/32$ — .46875		$31/32$ — .96875	
$1/2$ — .5		1 — 1.	

APPENDIX B

COMPOUND INTEREST

This table shows how your capital will grow if you reinvest all interest and dividends from your stocks or bonds. If, for example, you own $1,000 worth of a mutual fund which yields an average of 8 percent a year, at the end of the first year you will have $1,000 plus the 8 percent, or $80.00. Reinvesting the $80.00 in the fund gives you $1,080. At the end of the second year, your yearly 8 percent is figured on this new amount of $1,080 (instead of the original $1,000), giving you $86.40. Adding on this $86.40, you now have $1,166.40, the amount you will use in figuring your third year's interest. (On the table, $1,166.40 is rounded off to $1,166.)

This constant adding on of income is called "compounding," and the resulting growth of your capital is much greater than it would be with simple interest. For example, simple interest of $80.00 a year (8 percent of $1,000), would add up to $800 in 10 years. Adding that to your original $1,000 would give you a total of $1,800.

Compounding the interest, however, will give you a substantially larger figure. Refer to the chart under the 8 percent column. Follow the line for 10 years over to this column and you will see a figure of 2.158. This is the number you use to multiply the original $1,000 investment. $1,000 times 2.158 gives you $2,158, the amount you would have if you reinvested all your income each year.

The 2.158 is what is called the *multiplier*. No matter how much you invest and compound for 10 years, you would multiply it by 2.158 to arrive at your 10-year gain.

The advantage of compounding gets more dramatic as the years go by. At 20 years, the chart shows a figure of 4.660 under the 8 percent column. $1,000 times 4.660 = $4,660.

If you want to see real drama, though, look at how the compound interest increases as the average amount reinvested increases. Take a look at the 20 percent column. With an average income of 20 percent reinvested each year, $1,000 will grow to $6,191 after 10 years. And 20 years will show a whopping $38,337.

This table should give you some idea of why investing in small company stocks is a powerful way of increasing your investment capital. We are aiming for average yearly returns of 20 percent to 25 percent, and better. Although you may not reinvest any returns yearly, when you do sell a stock, reinvesting the original capital *and* any increase in value will allow you to compound your gains.

Please notice that we say "average" yearly returns. Some years, you may see very little increase, or even a minus, while other years will give you a very large gain. The table in Appendix C shows the great variations in performance from year to year of small company stocks as a whole.

A2. $1.00 Compounded Annually

Years	Annual Rate					Years
	5%	**6%**	**7%**	**8%**	**9%**	
1	$ 1.050	1.060	1.070	1.080	1.090	1
2	1.102	1.123	1.144	1.166	1.188	2
3	1.157	1.191	1.225	1.259	1.295	3
4	1.215	1.262	1.310	1.360	1.411	4
5	1.276	1.338	1.402	1.469	1.538	5
6	1.340	1.418	1.500	1.586	1.677	6
7	1.407	1.503	1.605	1.713	1.828	7
8	1.477	1.593	1.718	1.850	1.992	8
9	1.551	1.689	1.838	1.999	2.171	9
10	1.628	1.790	1.967	2.158	2.367	10
11	1.710	1.898	2.104	2.331	2.580	11
12	1.795	2.012	2.252	2.518	2.812	12
13	1.885	2.132	2.409	2.719	3.065	13
14	1.979	2.260	2.578	2.937	3.341	14
15	2.078	2.396	2.759	3.172	3.642	15
16	2.182	2.540	2.952	3.425	3.970	16
17	2.292	2.692	3.158	3.700	4.327	17
18	2.406	2.854	3.379	3.996	4.717	18
19	2.526	3.025	3.619	4.315	5.141	19
20	2.653	3.207	3.869	4.660	5.604	20
25	3.386	4.291	5.427	6.848	8.623	25
30	4.321	5.743	7.612	10.062	13.267	30

(continued)

A2. $1.00 COMPOUNDED ANNUALLY (CONTINUED)

Years		Annual Rate				Years
	10%	12%	15%	18%	20%	
1	1.100	1.120	1.150	1.180	1.200	1
2	1.210	1.254	1.322	1.392	1.440	2
3	1.331	1.404	1.520	1.643	1.728	3
4	1.464	1.573	1.749	1.938	2.073	4
5	1.610	1.762	2.011	2.287	2.488	5
6	1.771	1.973	2.313	2.699	2.985	6
7	1.948	2.210	2.660	3.185	3.583	7
8	2.143	2.475	3.059	3.758	4.299	8
9	2.357	2.773	3.517	4.435	5.159	9
10	2.593	3.105	4.145	5.233	6.191	10
11	2.853	3.478	4.652	6.175	7.430	11
12	3.138	3.895	5.350	7.287	8.916	12
13	3.452	4.363	6.152	8.599	10.699	13
14	3.797	4.887	7.075	10.147	12.839	14
15	4.177	5.473	8.137	11.973	15.407	15
16	4.594	6.130	9.357	14.149	18.488	16
17	5.054	6.866	10.751	16.672	22.186	17
18	5.559	7.689	12.375	19.673	26.623	18
19	6.115	8.612	14.231	23.214	31.948	19
20	6.727	9.646	16.366	27.393	38.337	20
25	10.834	17.000	32.918	62.668	95.396	25
30	17.449	29.959	66.211	143.370	237.376	30

APPENDIX C

THE HISTORICAL DIFFERENCE

This table combined with the table in Appendix B, should erase any lingering doubts you have about the advantage of investing in small stocks. The average yearly gain of small company stocks from 1974 to 1991 was 20.7 percent, while the average gain of the large S&P 500 companies was 14.7 percent.

Turn to Appendix B and follow the 15 percent column down to 17 years (we are rounding off 14.7 percent to 15 percent). There we find a multiplier of 10.751. $1,000 invested blue chips of the S&P 500 in 1974 would have grown to approximately $10,751 by 1991.

Now look at the 20 percent column (we are rounding off 20.7 percent to 20 percent). At 17 years, the multiplier is 22.186. $1,000 invested in small companies in 1974 would have grown to approximately $22,186 by 1991, more than twice as much as the returns from the larger stocks. In both cases, it is assumed that any gains from dividends or from buying and selling stocks would be reinvested.

As stated in chapter 1, these figures are for all small companies. The investor who carefully researches small firms before buying should realize even better profits than these averages.

A3. Total Rates of Return: Small Firms versus Large Firms

Year	Small Firm Stocks	S&P 500 Index	Difference Favoring Small Firms
1974	– 19.9	– 26.5	6.6
1975	52.8	37.2	15.6
1976	54.7	23.8	30.9
1977	25.4	– 7.2	32.6
1978	23.5	6.6	16.9
1979	43.5	18.4	25.1
1980	39.9	32.4	7.5
1981	13.9	– 4.9	18.8
1982	28.0	21.4	6.6
1983	39.7	22.5	17.2
1984	– 6.7	6.3	– 13.0
1985	24.7	32.2	– 7.5
1986	6.9	18.5	– 11.6
1987	– 9.3	5.2	– 14.5
1988	22.9	16.8	6.1
1989	10.2	31.5	– 21.3
1990	– 21.6	– 3.2	– 18.4
1991	44.6	30.5	14.1
Average	20.7%	14.5%	6.2%

Source: Roger G. Ibbotson and Rex Sinquefield, *Stocks, Bonds, Bills and Inflation: 1992 Yearbook.* (Chicago: Ibbotson Associates).

INDEX